London's Disused Railway Stations
Outer South East London

J. E. Connor

Capital Transport

Above: Eltham Park station, shortly before closure.

Title page: Coombe Road station, looking towards Selsdon on the last day of services in May 1983.

The author and publisher acknowledge the following photographers and collectors whose images have been reproduced in this book:
Ian Baker, C.F. Barnes, R.K. Blencowe, John Bradshaw, British Railways (Southern Region),
Roger Carpenter, H.C. Casserley, Nick Catford, J.E. Connor, John Crook, Croydon Local Studies Library,
Denis Cullum (Lens of Sutton Association), Alan A. Jackson, P. Laming, Lens of Sutton Association,
J. Minnis, Pamlin Prints, B.P. Pask, H.J. Patterson-Rutherford, Pictorial Times, A.M. Riley, R.C. Riley,
South Eastern & Chatham Railway Society, Southern Railway.

Contents

Introduction	4
The London Brighton & South Coast Railway	7
Norwood	8
Croydon Central	13
The London Chatham & Dover Railway	18
Honor Oak	19
Lordship Lane	26
Upper Sydenham	34
Crystal Palace High Level	42
Penge	60
The South Eastern Railway	62
Church Manorway Halt	63
Eltham Well Hall	65
Eltham Park	70
Chislehurst	79
Lower Sydenham	79
New Beckenham	80
Woodside	82
Addiscombe	92
Bingham Road	108
Coombe Road	124
Spencer Road Halt	138
Selsdon	142

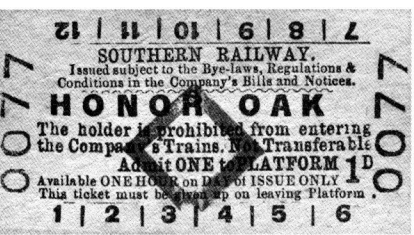

First published 2022

Published by Capital Transport Publishing
www.capitaltransport.com

Printed in the EU

© J. E. Connor 2022

Introduction

Many people of a certain age have a special affection for the 1960s and they look back over the decade with great nostalgia. Largely this revolves around the music and fashions of the era, but it was also a period of great change in others ways.

To us young railway enthusiasts, it meant the imminent demise of steam hauled services on British Rail and much of our time was spent scurrying around the country, photographing as much as we could before the old order disappeared for ever.

In 1964, I joined the Norbury & South London Transport Club, which, under the leadership of their visits organiser, Barry Sleath, arranged various *"shed bashes"* and also held regular meetings at St. Christopher's School, Thornton Heath.

I suppose that Thornton Heath was a fair distance from my home in Stepney Green, but it was an easy journey by Underground and Southern Electric and I attended their gatherings on a regular basis. As a member of *"The Norbury Club"* I made lots of new friends and, not surprisingly, the vast majority of these lived south of the Thames.

Around this time, I began to develop an interest in disused stations and lines and often incorporated these into my weekend trips using the fondly remembered Twin Rover tickets, which allowed unlimited travel on London Transport *"red buses"* and much of the Underground network.

In the summer of 1965, I left school and began working as an enquiry clerk at the Central Telephone Bureau, Waterloo. Before joining, I had the chance of similar positions closer to home, but Waterloo still had regular main line steam services with Bulleid pacifics in and out all day long, so it won hands down!

On our office wall was a large yellowing map of the London suburban network, and this included the old branch between Nunhead and Crystal Palace High Level. The line had closed when I was only five years old and, not surprisingly, I never travelled on it.

With my good friend, and fellow Norbury club member, Ian Baker, I set out to explore the route in October 1965. By this time I had become familiar with some of the closed stations in east London and was hoping to find similar survivals on this line. However, I was to be very disappointed. There were no splendid buildings still bearing the names of their pre-grouping owners, and no derelict stations rotting away on inaccessible elevated formations. All we found was an overgrown trackbed, and an unusual wooden footbridge above the cutting near Lordship Lane. Beyond here however, there were two tunnels and we walked through the first of these to reach the site of Upper Sydenham. I'd never walked through a tunnel before and found it a bit unnerving, but the thought of something of interest at the other end made it all worthwhile. Unfortunately, as we emerged into the bright daylight, all we found were two platforms that were so covered in foliage that they were hardly discernible!

Ian remembered seeing the huge branch terminus at Crystal Palace High Level in his younger days and recalled its subsequent demolition so, as its buildings had already gone, we decided to leave the line to its slumber and head off to visit the loco sheds at Willesden and Southall.

One of my colleagues at Waterloo had travelled on the special last train over the branch and still retained her ticket. She appreciated my fascination for such things and generously passed it over to me. She said that she hadn't been back since closure, so a few months after my first visit, we made our way over to Forest Hill and accessed the old trackbed, which we walked as far as the northern portal of Crescent Wood Tunnel. We didn't enter however but caught a bus to Crystal Palace instead. She knew that the station itself had gone, but the splendidly engineered brick-lined cutting was still there and, more intriguingly, the pedestrian subway which once linked the station to the 'Palace' on the opposite side of the Parade.

At the time I had no idea that this existed and, to be quite honest, without her I would not have found it so easily. These days the subway is, quite rightly, well fenced off, but back then it was accessible across a piece of wasteland which had been part of the old 'Palace' grounds. It seemed very ornate and impressive and I felt as though we were explorers discovering something that had been abandoned in far-off antiquity. However, in reality, the station had only closed less than twelve years earlier!

I may have missed seeing the branch when it was still functioning, but I made sure that I recorded the other routes in the area which closed later.

In some respects, the Woodside & South Croydon line, which succumbed in 1983, had similarities to the Palace branch, insomuch as it was part of the Southern Electric system and it passed through tunnels to the north of Coombe Road.

In its later days it was a fairly sad place, with all three stations looking rather down at heel. Bingham Road was still intact, but Coombe Road had lost its down side building and, apart from the signal box, the only structure at Selsdon was the grey-painted wooden hut which served as a booking office. Not that this ever seemed to be open when I visited however, although I gather it retained ticket stocks until the end.

Even on the run-up to closure, there were very few passengers but the friendly booking clerks at both Bingham Road and Coombe Road were happy to sell tickets to collectors from their Edmondson racks.

The final day was busier and the last train of all was packed with enthusiasts. Some time earlier my wife, Trish, had bought me a Super 8 cine camera with sound and I used this to record the view from the carriage window as we made our way towards Elmers End.

Talking of Elmers End, another line to close in more recent times was that which served Woodside and Addiscombe.

In the 1990s, my son Charlie and myself often travelled up to London on Saturdays and explored the railway network. Everything had changed greatly since my days at the Waterloo CTB back in 1965-6, but quite a few suburban lines on the South Eastern Division retained the slam door EPB units which, by then, were beginning to seem quite vintage.

One line which we included regularly was the branch to Addiscombe where, after a long day walking around taking photographs, the EPBs with their dusty but comfortable seats, always seemed so inviting. Having entered the station we would make our way onto the little concourse and invariably be greeted by the rhythmic thumping of the brake compressor of a unit standing at the buffer stops.

After closure, part of the route from Elmers End to Addiscombe was incorporated into the Croydon Tramlink system, along with some of the old Woodside & South Croydon so, in a way, they continue to serve the local area.

All these lines have their place in the history of London's railway network and I hope that you find them as fascinating as I have since I started to know them nearly sixty years ago.

Occasionally, the Woodside line was visited by railtours, particularly towards the end of Southern Region steam in the 1960s. On 5th March 1967, it was the turn of the Locomotive Club of Great Britain's *Surrey Downsman* special train, which reached the route by way of Longhedge Junction, Factory Junction, Brixton, Nunhead, Lewisham and Elmers End. During this stage of the journey it was headed by Bulleid West Country pacific No 34102 *Lapford*, although by this time her nameplates had been removed. Here the loco is seen at Selsdon where a ten minute photographic stop was made before proceeding to Oxted.

Introduction – 5

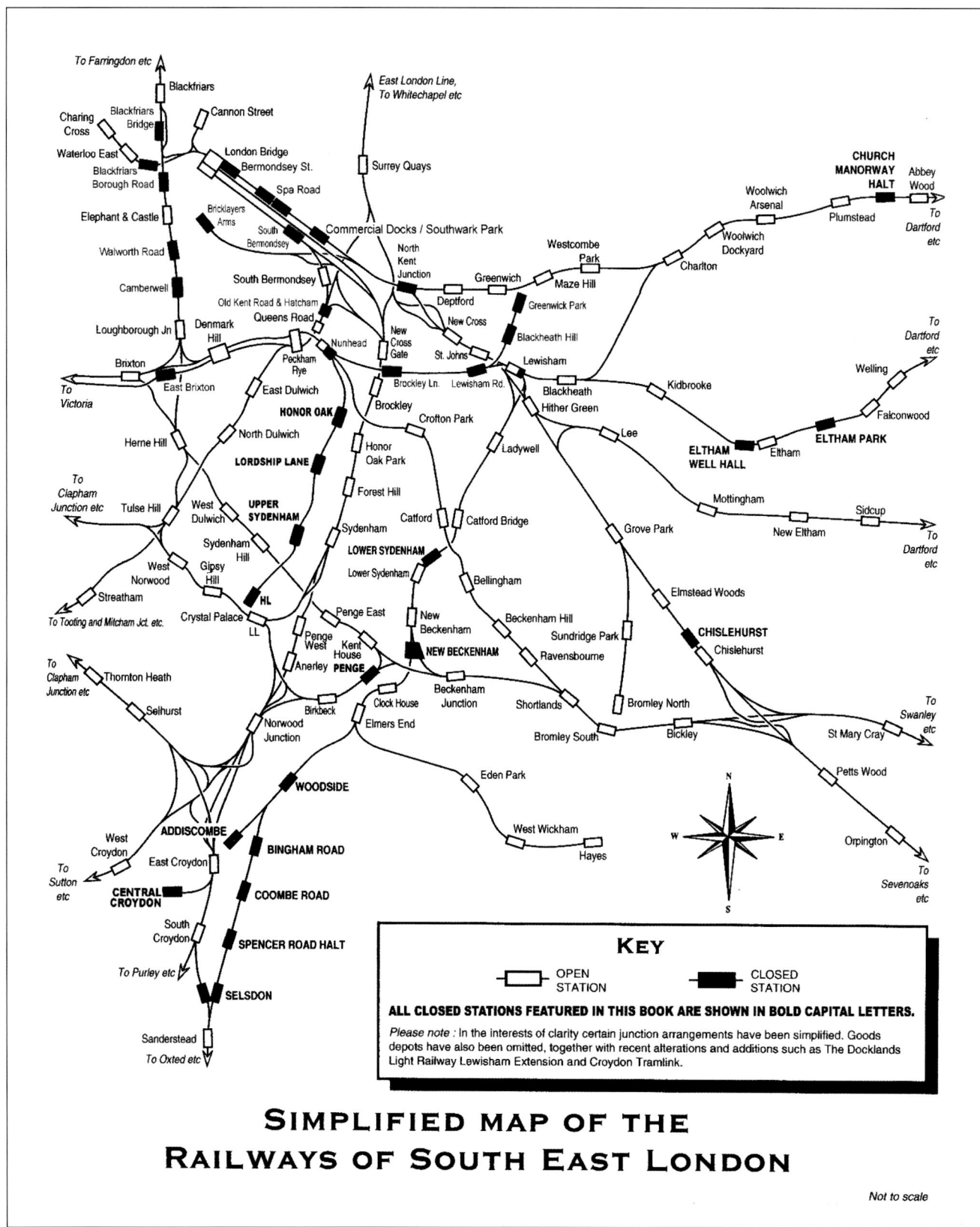

Simplified map of the Railways of South East London

Not to scale

The London Brighton & South Coast Railway

The late 1830s brought the advent of the London & Croydon Railway, which commenced at a junction with the Greenwich line near Corbett's Lane and terminated at the station now known as West Croydon.

This route, which opened throughout on 5th June 1839, had intermediate stations at New Cross, Dartmouth Arms, Sydenham, Penge, Anerley Bridge and Jolly Sailor. With the exception of Sydenham, all of these were subsequently renamed, including Jolly Sailor, which as 'Norwood' was closed and replaced by the present Norwood Junction in 1859.

While the LCR was still in its formative stage, the London & Brighton Railway acquired Parliamentary authority to build a line connecting Croydon with Brighton and other locations on the Sussex coast. Royal Assent was received on 15th July 1837 and work on the route, which joined the LCR south of Jolly Sailor, was duly put in hand. The section between Shoreham and Brighton opened on 12th May 1840, followed by Norwood - Haywards Heath on 12th July 1841 and the link from Haywards Heath to Brighton two months later on 21st September.

Following an Act of 27th July 1846, the LBR and LCR amalgamated and the resulting company became known as the London Brighton & South Coast Railway.

In 1853, a new company, the West End of London & Crystal Palace Railway, received powers to build a link between Crystal Palace and the London & South Western Railway at Wandsworth. A connection with the LBSCR was to be provided at Norwood, whilst at the northern end there would be a branch to Battersea Wharf, near Chelsea Bridge. An agreement with the LBSCR was reached during 1853 and it was decided that the line should be continued across the Thames to a terminus in London's West End. Negotiations to this end took place between the company and the LSWR, but the idea proved unpopular, so the South Western withdrew from the scheme in 1855.

Work on the route between Crystal Palace and Battersea Wharf duly commenced and the line opened to a temporary terminus at Wandsworth on 1st December 1856. The extension to Battersea Wharf, or 'Pimlico' as the company confusingly called it, followed on 29th March 1858, but the same year saw the sanctioning of the new cross-river section, so the Battersea terminus proved to be short-lived.

The northward extension was built by the Victoria Station & Pimlico Railway and the first stone of the new Thames bridge was laid on 9th June 1859. Since 1858, the WELCPR had been leased to the LBSCR and it was purchased outright the following year.

As with many companies serving the inner suburbs, the LBSCR suffered from tramway competition in the early twentieth century and responded by introducing electric trains over part of its network in 1909. The first section to be electrified was the South London Line, linking London Bridge with Victoria and other suburban routes followed. The company employed overhead wiring and may have been more extensive had it not been for the intervention of the First World War.

After the grouping in 1923, the newly formed Southern Railway decided that although suburban electrification was very desirable, they preferred the third rail system which was then in use on the LSWR. Following this decision, the wires on the former LBSCR were taken down and replaced by conductor rails, with the last of the overhead electrics running in the small hours of 22nd September 1929.

The closure notice for Central Croydon station as once displayed in the late, lamented Museum of British Transport at Clapham. The station had been renamed Croydon Central in 1886 but, for some reason, the poster showed its original title.

The London Brighton & South Coast Railway - 7

Norwood

Opened as Jolly-sailor (London & Croydon Railway): 5.6.1839.
Renamed Norwood (London & Croydon Railway): 1846.
Closed and replaced by Norwood Junction (London Brighton & South Coast Railway): 1.6.1859.

The name was originally (but not consistently) shown with the two words hyphenated and the 's' of sailor printed in lower case type. The station was sometimes referred to prior to renaming as 'Jolly-sailor, Norwood'; 'Jolly-sailor near Beaulah Spa' or 'Jolly-sailor near Beaulah Spa and that part of Norwood'.

The original station to serve Norwood was opened by the London & Croydon Railway on 5th June 1839 and was named 'Jolly-sailor' after a nearby public house.

According to *The Croydon Railway and its Adjacent Scenery* written by W.E. Trotter and published in 1839, it was located 72chains, 11 leagues south of Anerley and 1mile, 77chains, 88 leagues from what is now West Croydon.

The station stood to the north of a level crossing which took what is now Norwood Hill across the formation and its main building, located on the up side, was reached by means of a footpath. Mr Trotter's book gives us a contemporary description of the line as viewed from a train and his paragraph detailing Jolly-sailor commences at Goat House Bridge: *"Immediately beyond this bridge, as we emerge from the cutting, stands the Norwood station, a neat structure of brick with stone dressings, having on the north and south small wings, from which a colonnade of cast iron columns is continued round the west front. Nearly facing the station, on the opposite side of the railway, is a range of rustic cottages, intended to form dwellings for some of the servants of the company. At the southern boundary of this station the road from Norwood to Addington intersects the railway on the level; and here, as in all similar cases, danger is guarded against by gates, which are closed towards the road on the arrival of the train, and towards the railway so soon as the train has past."*

From this piece it is apparent that in the station's earliest days it was being referred to colloquially as *"Norwood"*, even if this was not yet its official name. A degree of indecision can also be found elsewhere in the publication, as a fares list on the back cover called it *"Jolly-sailor near Beulah Spa"* whilst a diagram showed *"Station, Norwood"* on a gradient of 1 in 660, falling towards Croydon. This diagram appeared on a large folding route map, which was included within the book and also detailed the various locations. The panel relevant to Norwood showed the premises as *"Jolly Sailors"*, therefore suggesting that the boisterous Jack Tar had been joined by all his mates!

Elsewhere in the publication, Mr Trotter's narrative described the surroundings: *"From the Jolly-sailor or Norwood-station, the former of which name has been derived from the proximity of a pleasantly situated public-house bearing that sign, a delightful walk of a mile brings us to the well-known Beaulah Spa which was established in the year 1831 as a place of elegant recreation for Londoners, and a resort for the numerous invalids who have been induced by the salubrity of the air and rural character of the locality to make Norwood and its vicinity their residence ... "*

At the time of opening, first and second class tickets from Jolly-sailor to London Bridge cost 1/9d and 1/3d respectively, whilst passengers could book to Croydon for 9d or 6d, again depending on class of travel.

Within a short time, local people were beginning to get concerned over the possible dangers of the adjoining level crossing and requested that it should be replaced by a *"tunnel under the line"*. This was no doubt a good idea, as the road was widely used by both pedestrians and horse-drawn traffic, but neither the LCR or the local council wanted to finance the scheme, so despite various suggestions, there was little progress. On 6th November 1841, the Croydon Board of Highways wrote to the railway offices at 205 Tooley Street: *"Your letter of 3rd instant, containing proposals that the surveyors of the Board of Highways of this parish should undertake to make the tunnel under the railroad at the Jolly Sailor station at Norwood, upon receiving from the London and Croydon Railway Company the sum of £1000 towards the cost of it, is a proposition that cannot upon any principal or reason be entertained for a moment ... At the same time the Board consider the making of the tunnel by your Company is the only method of insuring the satisfaction of the parishioners and the public, and they earnestly hope that the work will be proceeded with as the best mode of avoiding the danger incidental to the crossing in question."* From surviving records it seems that the correspondence regarding this matter continued until 19th November 1841, but although further details are sketchy it is known that the road was subsequently lowered and a railway bridge was built to replace the level crossing.

At a meeting of the London & Croydon Board of Directors on 22nd September 1842, it was stated that detailed tenders were being prepared by the engineer, Charles Hutton Gregory, for *"repairs at the Jolly Sailor"*, but the nature of these does not seem to have been recorded.

More obvious changes were to come within a few years however, as in August 1844, the LCR received Parliamentary authority to convert part of its system to atmospheric propulsion and one of the stationary engine houses was to be erected on the down side at Jolly Sailor station.

Jolly-sailor station in 1845, showing the ornate atmospheric railway pump-house, designed by W.H. Brakespear and Raphael Brandon, at centre. Beyond it, to the left is the Goat House bridge, which was named after a nearby hotel, whilst alongside the platform can be seen an artist's impression of an atmospheric train.

So that the plan could proceed, the formation between Dartmouth Arms (now Forest Hill) and Croydon had to be widened and a third track laid with a 15in diameter cast iron traction pipe between the running rails. Space restrictions preclude a detailed description of how the system worked, but suffice to say that each train was hauled by a special carriage with under-floor apparatus. This projected downwards through a valve-operated longitudinal slot along the top of an otherwise airtight tube and ended at a piston. As the stationary pumping engines created a vacuum by exhausting the air ahead of this piston, the atmospheric pressure to the rear propelled the train and fairly high speeds could be attained. For a while, the atmospheric principle was promoted as a viable alternative to steam locomotives, but it was an experiment doomed to failure.

The idea had been sold to the LCR back in August 1840, by the firm of Messrs Samuda Bros, who suggested that it would be a more efficient way of working the section on New Cross bank, than by the locomotives then employed. The LCR Directors consulted their own engineer, William Cubitt, along with John Urpeth Rastrick of the London & Brighton Railway, and it seems to have met with the approval of both men. It was originally intended to continue the atmospheric system into London Bridge and southwards to Epsom, but these extensions were not to be.

Apart from the widening, the most significant engineering work was the world's first railway flyover, which had to be constructed south of Jolly-sailor to carry the atmospheric line above the conventional 'Brighton' tracks below. As this was not intended for locomotive use, it was built as a timber trestle and featured stiff 1 in 50 gradients at either end.

Three pumping stations were initially provided, with installations at Croydon and Dartmouth Arms in addition

Norwood – 9

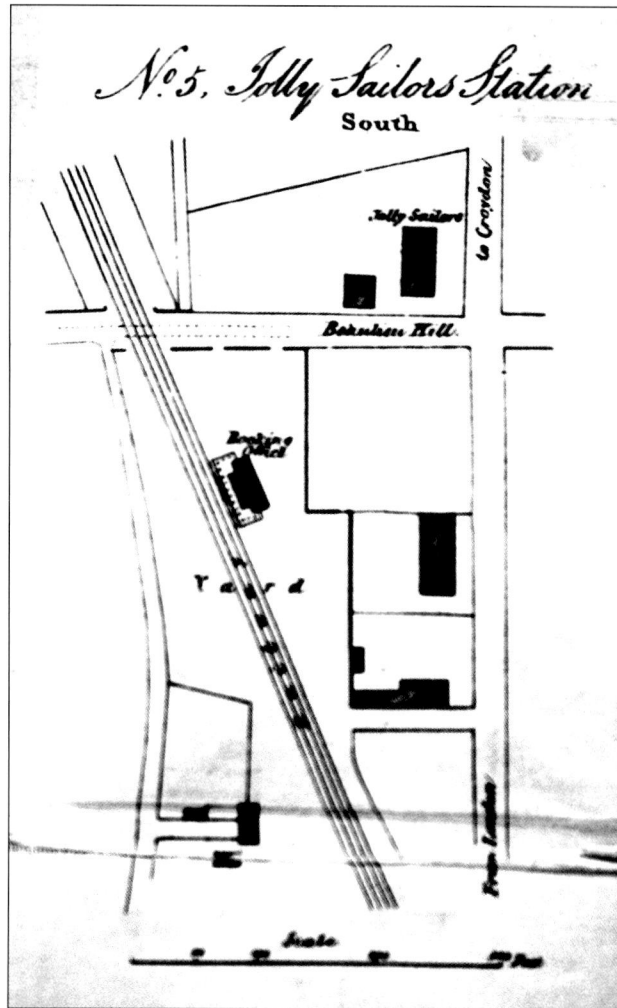

A map included in W.E. Trotter's 1839 book *The Croydon Railway and its Adjacent Scenery*, showing the location of the station. Confusingly, south is at the top, whilst north is at the bottom. The booking office is shown on the up side, along with what appears to represent a short platform. The *Jolly Sailor(s)* public house appears near the top right. The map was scanned from a poor photocopy and sadly leaves much to be desired!

to that at Jolly-sailor. To appease local objectors, the buildings were designed in a gothic style reminiscent of imaginary churches and featured tall ornate chimneys, which also served as outlets for the exhausted air. The work was credited to the LCR architect, W.H. Brakespear, although it is understood that the ornamental detailing was carried out by Raphael Brandon, a noted architect, who seemingly only received £30 in payment. In August 1845, *The Pictorial Times* gave this glowing description of the buildings: *"The engine-houses are the most beautiful things of their kind that have ever been erected in this country. They are the work of Mr W.H. Brakespear the Architect, and his object has been to show that the most uncouth forms may be so decorated as to become ornaments to the landscape. Without going into details we may mention that the boiler fires being on the smoke-consuming principle, a strong draft is necessary for their maintenance, which can only be obtained by a tall chimney or "stalk" as manufacturers term it. But a chimney being a most unsightly object, and many of them being wanted on the course of an atmospheric line, to the certain annoyance of gentlemen through whose grounds the railway would pass, it was determined that they should receive at the hands of the builder such an amount of architectural direction as would make them objects of interest rather than eyesores."*

The engines themselves were supplied by Maudslay, Son & Field and were all coal fired. Their fuel was delivered by rail to adjoining sidings and the installation at Jolly-sailor was equipped with its own atmospheric powered 10ton crane which was used to off-load incoming wagons. The crane was supplied by the firm of Fox & Henderson and cost the company £250.

On 13th September 1845, *Herapath's Journal* reported that the atmospheric line of the LCR *"runs parallel with the locomotive line; and connected with it three pairs of engines for exhausting the tubes have already been erected; the first at the Croydon station; the second at the Norwood station, a little more than two miles from Croydon; and the third at the Dartmouth Arms, three miles from the Norwood station. The engines are of 50 horse power each. From Croydon to Norwood the trains are propelled by the Norwood engine which exhausts the first two miles of pipe, and afterwards the duty of exhaustion for the remaining three miles is taken up by the Dartmouth Arms engine, which actuates the train to that station. On returning from the Dartmouth Arms the vacuum is created for the first three miles as far as the Norwood station by the engine at that place, and for the rest of the distance by the engine fixed there..."*

At the beginning of November 1845, the installations were inspected on behalf of the Board of Trade by Major-General Sir Charles Pasley FRS and *The Times* reported: *"The weather being fine, the return of the train to town was delayed for the purpose of giving the company an opportunity of inspecting the stationary engine and air-pump, manufactured by the eminent firm of Maudslay, Son and Field, and of which very many availed themselves. At a minute and a half to three the train started from Croydon on its return and entered the atmospheric pipe at forty seconds before three. In the first minute it reached a speed of 16 miles an hour and in the second about 28 miles an hour. At the Norwood station the train was stopped for a short period but was started again at four minutes and fifty seconds past three... Great crowds of well-dressed persons congregated about the various points along the line from which a glance of the passing trains might be caught, and not a few of them seemed to be much astonished at the velocity obtained in the apparent absence of any motive power."*

Major-General Pasley was suitably impressed and officially sanctioned the system a few days later.

What is understood to have been the Jolly-sailor station house can be seen near the centre of this view, whilst the present Norwood Junction appears to the left. The date of demolition has not been traced, but it is thought that the old building survived into the 1960s.

A pre-grouping view, taken from the north end of Norwood Junction, with the 'Jolly-sailor building' partially hidden by the signal box to the right of the nameboard.
The name shown on the board, Norwood Junction & South Norwood for Woodside, was carried from 1st October 1910 until 13th June 1955.

Unfortunately, the LCR venture into atmospheric propulsion began to suffer problems from the outset and even its ornate pumping stations began to show defects. Soon after commissioning, it became apparent that their foundations were insufficient to withstand the vibration of the engines, and they had to be strengthened with bearing girders and additional brickwork. Around the same time, *"the conical spire of the Norwood Engine House"* was deemed dangerous and the contractors responsible for its construction, Grissell & Peto, were called back to make it safe.

Whereas the contemporary railway press were generally supportive of the scheme, the same could not be said of *Herapath's Journal*, which under the

Norwood – 11

heading *"Pulling down the churches alias the steam engine houses"* sarcastically stated on 8th November 1845: *"We understand that it is denied by Mr Samuda and his friends that the steeples of these buildings are taking down to prevent their falling, but because they do not give draught enough. This reason is more strange than ours. We have been taught, as the universal result of experience, that high chimneys very much improve the draught. It is, however, quite evident now that we, and all the world beside, are wrong. Mr Brunel was to inspect the works yesterday, when it was fully expected that the two geniuses, Brunel and Samuda, intended to prescribe new rules and new laws for Dame Nature, from which, under severe penalties, she was to depart. One of them, it is supposed, was that henceforth labour and expense are not to be directly but inversely proportional to the work done; a second that the air is to have less than no friction in passing through tubes; and a third, the most important of all - that chimnies* (sic)*, if they fall from excessive vibration of the engines, should fall upwards and lodge in the clouds."*

Sarcasm aside, *Herapath* was perhaps right to doubt the suitability of atmospheric operation as the LCR was soon to find. There was no doubt that, when working properly, it offered better acceleration and higher speeds than were generally achievable with locomotives of the period, but there were many drawbacks not present on conventional railways. Special pointwork had to be designed to enable run-rounds at termini and escaping air was a constant problem.

Leaking pipes were often the cause of operating difficulties, although not all reported incidents were necessarily serious. In 1846, a writer described how he saw a woman drop her handkerchief on the track whilst waiting on the platform at Jolly-sailor. As it fell towards the sleepers, it suddenly gained momentum then disappeared completely as it got sucked into the tube.

After so many years of inconsistency regarding the station's title, Jolly-sailor was officially renamed Norwood in 1846, but the active life of its adjoining pump-house was drawing to a close.

When the LCR became one of the constituent companies of the LBSCR in the summer of 1846, the new management endeavoured to continue with the atmospheric system, but seemingly had little faith in it. The cast-iron traction pipe was continued between the rails from Forest Hill to New Cross early the following year, but although everything performed well, there would be no further work carried out and the remaining planned extensions were scrapped. An additional engine house had been erected at New Cross, but this did not prove necessary. The end came in early May 1847, when the LBSCR gave up the idea of atmospheric propulsion and converted the line to ordinary locomotive haulage. The Company had no doubt made the right choice and quickly set about removing the equipment. As there was now no need to keep the two systems separate, the timber flyover near Norwood was rendered redundant and hastily demolished, but the pump houses remained standing.

In his now familiar sarcastic tone reserved for all things atmospheric, John Herapath wrote in his *Journal*: *"We have been asked, what will be done with the four engine houses, alias churches on the Croydon line? It has been suggested that Mr Wilkinson* (of the LCR) *takes one to live in; Mr Samuda another; and that the two others be made a church and a synagogue for them to pray daily in, for the sin of wasting so much of innocent Shareholders' money."*

The engine house at Norwood seems to have been abandoned completely, as a pencil sketch by Thomas Noakes made in 1853 and now in the Local Studies Department at Croydon Library, shows the building as though it was derelict. Of course it is difficult to comment on its accuracy, but with two of its doors seemingly missing and what appears to be fallen masonry in the foreground, it resembles the type of gothic ruin which was sometimes romanticised in Victorian art. Interestingly however, the chimney appears to be intact and not shortened in any way, as inferred by *Herapath's Journal*. The date of its demolition has not been confirmed, but it is thought to have gone by 1861.

Back on 23rd July 1849, a new small booking office was authorised at the station, whilst a little over three years later, on 4th October 1852, a tender from R. Bushby for constructing a *"new station and cottages"* at a cost of £2,350 was also approved.

This rebuilding presumably did not go ahead, but changes to the local railway network certainly brought the need for larger premises. The advent of the Norwood Spur proved to be the catalyst and, on 22nd July 1858, it was reported that *"Mr Francis Fuller attended the* (LBSCR) *Board and submitted a plan showing the Land for which he had been in negotiation for the new Station at Norwood. Mr Fuller was finally authorised to complete the purchase and it was Resolved that he should prepare and submit without delay a plan showing the manner in which he prepares to construct the Junction Station at Norwood."* A few weeks later, on 5th August, a set of general plans were submitted to the Board and these proved largely acceptable. The platforms and earthworks were to be constructed by the Company, but *"the station buildings and roof, etc"* were to be built by contractors and a selection of firms were invited to submit estimates. Some of the final details were still *"subject to certain unimportant alterations"* but following a site visit by the LBSCR Chairman towards the end of the following month, the new station plans met with full approval. Work seems to have started soon after and, on 1st June 1859, Norwood Junction was opened to traffic and its predecessor, which lay about 80 yards to the north was closed. After twenty eventful years, the station followed Samuda's atmospheric system into obscurity.

Croydon Central

Opened as Central Croydon (London Brighton & South Coast Railway): 1.1.1868.
Temporarily closed (London Brighton & South Coast Railway): 1.12.1871.
Reopened as Croydon Central (London Brighton & South Coast Railway): 1.6.1886.
Closed: 1.9.1890.

Croydon Central station boasted an attractive main building, constructed in a style favoured by the LBSCR at the time. This view looks down from the south side of Katharine Street and shows the forecourt and frontage.

In 1864, the LBSCR obtained powers to construct a short branch to link its suburban network with the centre of Croydon. This was to diverge beyond the south end of the present East Croydon station and terminate on the south side of Katharine Street.

The branch was double track throughout and extended for a distance of 29 chains. From the junction it descended on a gradient of 1 in 143 and, after passing beneath Park Lane, reached the terminus. This was known as Central Croydon and comprised four roads, although only the outer pair were served by platforms. Those in the centre provided runround facilities for locomotives and could also be used, if required, for stock storage. The main building stood at right angles to Katharine Street and included a double storey stationmaster's house at its northern end. The entrance was fronted by a small cab yard, whilst a double flight of steps provided access from the booking hall to both platforms.

Another photograph taken from Katharine Street, but this time showing the nameboard in full and including the rear of the platform buildings to the left.

Plans for the branch had been approved on 23rd September 1861 and the contract for its construction was let to William Pickering on 29th November 1864. A tender of £4,089 to build the terminus was submitted separately by John Thomas Chappell and accepted on 28th November 1865.

At the LBSCR Traffic Committee meeting of 22nd August 1867 it was announced that the station had been completed and that it should be opened immediately. A few weeks later, on 11th September, the company wrote to the Board of Trade and stated that it intended to commence services within a month. However, it seems that there was no response, as another letter was sent on 26th September repeating the information, but this time stating that traffic would begin in ten days.

Unfortunately, the LBSCR was rather premature with its proposed opening date, as when Central Croydon was eventually inspected, it fell a little short of Board of Trade requirements. In a report dated 15th October 1867, the inspecting officer, Lieutenant-Colonel F.H. Rich, wrote: *"The junction signals require adjusting to make them work smoothly"* and because of this, the line could not be opened to the public.

The improvements were subsequently made and the company again wrote to the BoT on 5th November. In a separate letter, posted the same day, the LBSCR said that it would like to bring the branch into use by 1st January 1868 and asked the Board of Trade if inspection could be deferred until 28th November to allow the installation of locking apparatus.

Station staff pose for the photographer beneath the entrance canopy. Although the date is unknown, the view was possibly taken in 1890, as what appears to be a closure notice, similar to that reproduced on page 7, can be seen at the left-hand end of the foreground posters. The station had been officially known as Croydon Central since 1886, but the earlier name continued to appear on the exterior sign and on the poster. Therefore it seems that despite the official renaming, the original title generally remained in use, although "Croydon (Central)" is known to have been printed on tickets.

Lt. Col. Rich duly returned on the suggested date, but was still dissatisfied with the progress. His report recorded: *"The points of the ballast siding near the junction with the South Croydon line have not yet been locked with the junction signals and a signal is required for the ballast siding. The spring buffers are not yet fixed at the end of the Central Station. I (feel) that the Central Croydon Station and Railway cannot be opened without danger to the public using the same in respect of the incompleteness of works."*

More alterations were carried out and on 19th December, the LBSCR told the Board of Trade that the line was ready for further inspection. Lt. Col. Rich therefore made his third visit and this time agreed that it was fit for opening, although he was still not totally happy with the signalling arrangements. He wrote: *"The locking apparatus at the entrance to the Central station is of a new Description, and is defective in the following points:- 1st That a part of the machinery has to be moved separately, with the hand or foot, which is awkward. 2nd The Signalman should be unable to lower the signals for the approach of a Train, until after he has set the points in the proper direction for it to pass. The Description of Locking Apparatus used at the Central Station should not be put up again, unless the above stated Defects can be altered."*

Presumably the company took note of these observations and subsequently acted upon them, although probably not prior to the branch opening.

Central Croydon was brought into use on 1st January

1868 with a weekday service of thirteen trains to London Bridge and twelve in the opposite direction. Most of these called at all intermediate stations and took around thirty-eight or forty minutes to complete their journeys. In addition, there were three up and four down workings linking the new terminus with Kensington Addison Road. These ran by way of Norwood Junction and Crystal Palace and again called at most places en route.

The Sunday service however was frugal to say the least, with just two up and one down on the London Bridge run and three turning round at Clapham Junction.

Mr S. Clarke was appointed as stationmaster on 10th January 1868, but from the outset it seems that Central Croydon was little used. However, 1869 brought some additional trains, when an existing LNWR Euston - New Croydon service was taken over by the LBSCR and amended to operate between Kensington and Central Croydon. Two of these workings made only two calls en route and therefore cut the journey time to thirty-one minutes.

Sadly the station was to prove unpopular and within four years of opening it seemed destined for an early demise. On 4th November 1871 the *Croydon Advertiser* reported: *"This month's timetables show a further reduction of the trains daily in and out of this station. There are now only three trains left, viz, the 11.30am the 3.06pm and the 4.20pm to London Bridge and the 10.05am, 1.32pm and 3.40pm from London Bridge. There are no trains to Victoria, but the 4.19pm from that station, which calls at Crystal Palace, is allowed by special favour to run into Central Station. The next reduction will be the closing of the station altogether."* The *Croydon Advertiser* was perfectly correct in this assumption and after the last train on 30th November 1871, all services were withdrawn.

The premises remained dormant for over a decade, but eventually the LBSCR gave in to local pressure and agreed that they should be brought back into use. Various alterations proved necessary and once these had been carried out the company informed the Board of Trade of its intentions.

This is the only photograph known to the author which shows the station platforms. As can be seen, steps led down from the booking hall and two locomotive release roads were provided.

Major General C. S. Hutchinson was appointed to make the inspection and his report dated 13th November 1885 stated: *"This station which has been closed for several years is about to be reopened and has been provided with modern signal arrangements and raised platforms etc. A new signal cabin has been erected containing 40 levers, of which 14 are at present spare. The station buildings were originally commodious and have not needed improvement."* Major General Hutchinson was less satisfied with certain other aspects however and he insisted on ten alterations being made to the pointwork and signalling before he could sanction reopening.

The station was nevertheless brought back into use on 1st June 1886, having had its name amended to Croydon Central. Three months later the LBSCR informed the Board of Trade that all its requirements had been complied with.

Despite the enthusiasm of the local authorities to have Croydon Central reopened, there again seemed little demand and by noon on the first day of its new lease of life, ticket sales had provided just 4d in revenue.

The LBSCR operated a single working from Croydon Central to Victoria, but apart from this the service was largely provided by the LNWR. Trains ran to and from Willesden Junction and, having called at the majority of intermediate stations, took around fifty-five minutes to make the journey.

From 1st February 1887, the Great Eastern service from Liverpool Street to New Cross via the East London Line was extended to Croydon Central and thus provided seven additional weekday trains in each direction.

Back in the 1860s, the station was largely served by indigenous LBSCR 2-4-0Ts of a type designed under John Chester Craven. There was more variety after reopening however, as locomotives belonging to both the GER and LNWR regularly worked in on their respective company's trains.

Unfortunately passengers preferred to use other stations in the locality and the terminus remained poorly patronised.

A closure date of 1st September 1890 was announced and the previous week's *Croydon Advertiser* suggested that if anybody wanted to take a last look around the station they had better do so before it was too late. After closure, the site was sold to the local Corporation for the erection of a new town hall.

The Ordnance Survey map of 1894-5 shows the branch tracks continuing a little to the west of Park Lane bridge, but although the station signal box appeared to be still standing, the terminus site beyond was undergoing redevelopment. Work on this had started in 1892 and took four years to complete. The new complex, which included not only the town hall, but a library and public gardens, was subsequently brought into use and Croydon Central station became largely forgotten.

The tracks between the junction and Park Lane were retained however and were used to serve an engineers' depot known as Fairfield Yard. Around 1931, the formation beneath Park Lane bridge was filled in, but the depot remained in use a little longer before succumbing to closure in February 1933. Two months later, the remaining section of the branch was auctioned and sold to the local council. The trackbed was buried and later used as a car park, but the site of the former junction remained just about discernable.

On 19th August 1949, the *Croydon Advertiser* included a photograph of a shed behind the Town Hall, which was claimed to be the last surviving remnant of the station itself. Unfortunately, the view had been taken in strong sunlight, so much of the building was in shadow, but a short length of canopy valancing indicated that it may have had railway origins. However, comparison with the only known platform view of Croydon Central shows that the valance designs differed, and the supporting post appeared to be wooden, whereas they were of iron on the station. This is not to say that the Town Hall *'shed'* was never part of the old premises, but from current photographic evidence it seems unlikely.

The car park lasted into the 1960s, when it was removed during the construction of Fairfield Halls and adjoining new buildings. A section of railway retaining wall on the northern side of the Town Hall Gardens still survives however and in comparatively recent years was fitted with a commemorative plaque. Apart from this, the branch which once served Croydon Central has vanished without trace.

The truncated remains of the Croydon Central branch, looking towards the buffer stops and the Town Hall Gardens in the final days of Fairfield Yard.

The London Chatham & Dover Railway

Originally known as the East Kent Railway, the LCDR did not receive its more familiar title until 1859, after its extension to London had been sanctioned.

Never the most affluent of organisations, its financial situation fell to an all-time low in the 1860s and led to a period in Chancery.

Its long-standing rivalry with the South Eastern Railway sometimes resulted in the construction of lines in areas already served by the SER, but ventures such as this taxed finances, which were already far from healthy.

Eventually, it became obvious that the rivalry was doing neither the LCDR nor SER any good, so an agreement was reached whereby the two companies would be managed by a joint committee. Parliamentary sanction for this was received in August 1899, although the working union actually came into operation at the beginning of that year.

The companies officially retained their individual identities, but were now managed and worked as the South Eastern & Chatham Railway. This situation continued until the grouping of 1923, when the system was absorbed into the newly formed Southern Railway.

The present listing contains all the LCDR stations in suburban south-east London, south of Nunhead, which have been abandoned.

The public footbridge over the former Crystal Palace High Level branch at Cox's Walk, looking towards the site of Lordship Lane station in the late 1960s.

Honor Oak

Opened (Crystal Palace & South London Junction Railway / London Chatham & Dover Railway): 12.1865.
Temporarily Closed (South Eastern & Chatham Railway): 1.1.1917 - 1. 3.1919.
and 22.5.1944 - 4.3.1946 (Southern Railway).
Closed (British Railways, Southern Region): 20.9.1954

Honor Oak station looking towards Nunhead in 1922.

The second intermediate station to be opened on the line between Nunhead and Crystal Palace, Honor Oak adjoined the eastern boundary of Camberwell Cemetery.

The wooden street level building was located east of the line and included a booking hall and waiting room. It was reached by means of a short approach from the south side of West Hill Road and was linked to a subway beneath the tracks by a covered path. From this subway, stairs ascended to the platforms, which were again constructed of wood.

Apart from the terminus at Crystal Palace, Honor Oak was the only location on the branch to be provided with goods facilities. These took the form of a small yard on the up side, south of the station. To operate the points leading to this, together with a crossover between the two passenger tracks, a thirteen lever signal box was erected a little beyond the country end of the down platform.

One of the station booking clerks made a grisly discovery in 1911, when he found the body of a political lecturer in a toilet, having committed suicide.

The sidings were extended in 1924 and a year later the down platform of the station was lengthened in concrete at its southern end prior to the introduction of electric services. At the same time, the earlier crossover was lifted and a replacement laid a little further south.

Passenger traffic had been in decline since around 1907, when people began to forsake the station in favour of new London County Council tramway services. Unfortunately electrification of the branch did not bring the hoped-for increase in traffic, as a census taken in February 1926 recorded only 654 passengers joining up trains and 560 alighting from those travelling towards Crystal Palace. Nevertheless the Southern Railway continued with improvements and a passimeter booth was authorised for Honor Oak in 1929.

The street level ticket office is thought to have closed in the 1930s, when new facilities were provided at platform level. By then the station boasted only a single member of staff, who sufficed as booking clerk, ticket collector and porter. As up and down services often pulled in simultaneously, the man on duty would sometimes cross to the opposite platform by opening the off-side doors and stepping from one train to the other.

Honor Oak suffered the same fate as the other stations on the Crystal Palace High Level branch and was twice closed due to wartime conditions. During the Second World War, the subway was fitted out with bunks and used as an air raid shelter, with brick screens being erected at either end in an attempt to give more protection from blasts.

Regular services ceased after traffic on Saturday 18th September 1954, but a special farewell steam train called at Honor Oak in both directions on the following day. At around the same time, a daily goods working from Herne Hill, which delivered coal to the yards, both here and at Crystal Palace, was also withdrawn, and the branch fell into complete disuse.

The station remained standing for around two years after closure, with demolition commencing just prior to track lifting. Being built almost entirely of wood, it was soon swept away. The concrete extension to the down platform, together with the adjoining signal box out-lived the remainder, but the box probably went soon after. By the later 1960s, all trace of Honor Oak station had gone, although the embankment on which it once stood still existed. This was subsequently removed and the site has since been developed for housing.

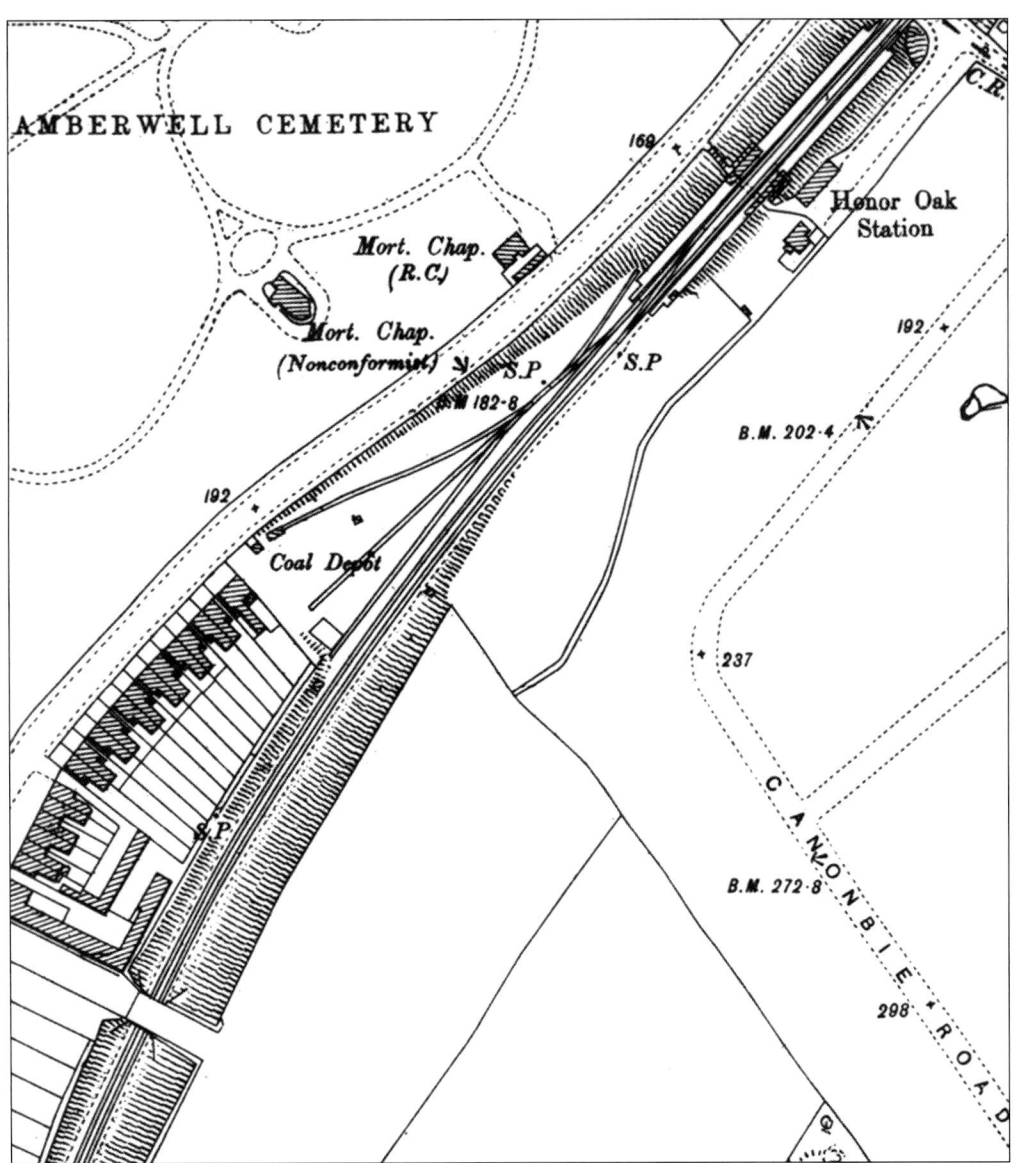

Extract from the 1:2500 Ordnance Survey of 1894 showing Honor Oak station and its adjoining coal depot. According to H.V. Borley's *Chronology of London Railways*, this opened with the station in December 1865. However, its absence from the 25in Ordnance Survey map of 1870 suggests a later date. It closed from 20th September 1954.

20 – London's Disused Railway Stations – Outer South East London

Above: Ex Great Northern Railway Class N1 0-6-2T No 4561 heads an excursion formed of LNER stock into Honor Oak station in October 1934.

Below: Honor Oak station looking towards Nunhead on 17th September 1954, which was the penultimate day of regular services over the line.

Above: Towards the end of the station's days, the wooden street level building became very dilapidated. Although undated, this view is thought to have been taken around the time of closure.

Left: Looking south from the down platform on 17th September 1954, with the signal box on the left and the goods yard to the right. The box was erected sometime between 1894 and 1914 to replace an earlier cabin which stood a little to its north-east.

Opposite top: Honor Oak station, as viewed from the goods yard around 1954.

Right: The north end of the station is seen on 17th September 1954, with the 4.37pm Blackfriars to Crystal Palace High Level arriving at the down platform.

Honor Oak – 23

Right: After closure, the street level building was boarded-up to deter further vandalism and is seen here, with the former station master's house on the left.

Below: The disused Honor Oak station, looking in the direction of Nunhead from the goods yard in April 1957, after the conductor rails had been lifted.

Above: The former up platform is seen, looking towards Nunhead during demolition.

Below: The remains of the station in 1964, after all but the 1925 concrete extension of the down platform had disappeared.

Lordship Lane

Opened (Crystal Palace & South London Junction Railway / London Chatham & Dover Railway): 1.9.1865.
Temporarily Closed (South Eastern & Chatham Railway): 1.1.1917 - 1.3.1919.
and 22.5.1944 - 4.3.1946 (Southern Railway).
Closed (British Railways, Southern Region): 20.9.1954

A train for Crystal Palace is seen from the Cox's Walk footbridge as it leaves Lordship Lane in pre-grouping days. The view is very similar to that portrayed in Camille Pissarro's 1871 painting, which is currently displayed in the Courtauld Institute Gallery, London. According to the 25in Ordnance Survey map of 1870, two sidings were provided at the Crystal Palace end of the station, although by 1893/4 only one of these remained and this is seen to the left of the photograph. They do not seem to have had any public access and are thought to have been for railway use only. It is understood that the surviving siding was lifted when the branch was electrified in the 1920s.

The first intermediate station to be opened on the Crystal Palace High Level branch, its entrance was reached by a short approach from the south side of Lordship Lane, just west of the junction with Sydenham Hill.

The Crystal Palace & South London Junction Railway, which was responsible for its construction, intended the station to open with the line, but there were delays in completion, so on 14th July 1865, the company informed the Board of Trade that it would not be ready in time. The route was brought into use a few weeks later on 1st August, then on 22nd August, the CP&SLJR again contacted the BoT, but this time to say that the building work at Lordship Lane had been finished.

Captain Rich carried out the inspection and stated in his report that it was *"sufficiently completed to be used for passenger traffic without danger to the public"*. The report was written on 1st September 1865 and the following day, the Board of Trade officially confirmed that all was well, although by then, trains had already started to call!

The main building was designed by Charles Barry to meet the aesthetic requirements of the Dulwich College Estate governors and stood to a height of two storeys. The ticket office was located at street level and a flight of stairs ascended to the down platform, which was constructed largely of wood. The same material was used for the up side, which was reached by means of a short subway beneath the tracks. The platforms were covered for part of their length by awnings and the up side was provided with a waiting shelter.

In 1871 Lordship Lane was used as the subject of a painting by the impressionist artist, Camille Pissarro, who chose a viewpoint, looking down onto the tracks from the Cox's Walk footbridge, a little south of the station.

A signal box was located at the country end of the down platform since at least 1870, but this was subsequently replaced by a newer cabin a little further south sometime between 1893 and 1914. The later box ceased to function in 1924, but it remained standing for the rest of the station's existence, possibly for the use of permanent way staff. The platforms were extended in concrete towards the box in readiness for electrification, but otherwise Lordship Lane was little altered until receiving air-raid damage in 1944.

The branch was closed for periods during both world wars, and its final demise in 1954 was perhaps inevitable. Towards the end, Lordship Lane presented a sorry sight, with its platform awnings gone and its main building displaying the scars of war. A poster was displayed near the former entrance directing any intending passengers to the nearby ex-LBSCR station at Forest Hill, which was described as being a five-minute walk away. Demolition came in March 1957 and the site was subsequently redeveloped for housing.

RIGHT: Lordship Lane station, looking towards Nunhead in Southern Railway days after the line was electrified.

Below: Extract from the 1:2500 Ordnance Survey map of 1893-4, showing the station near top left. To the south of here, the line went into cutting and was crossed by the Cox's Walk footbridge, which is seen near the bottom left.
In the upper part of the extract, to the right, appears the well-known Horniman Museum.

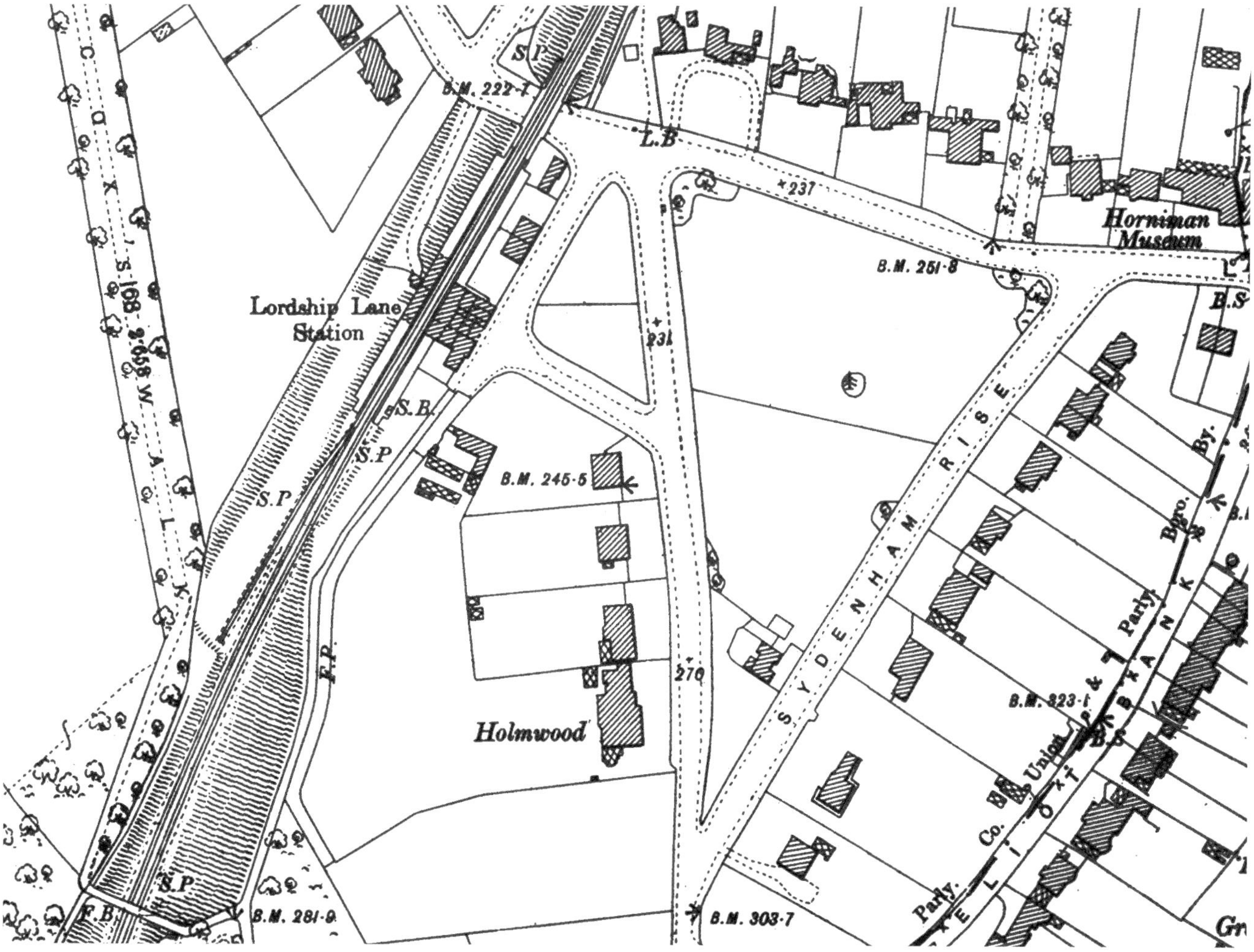

Lordship Lane – 27

Lordship Lane station suffered air raid damage twice in 1944, although fortunately, it was closed at the time. The first incident occurred at 6.45am on the morning of 6th July. According to the report, the station buildings were damaged and there was debris on the track. The next attack came at 10.20am on 1st August, when a V1 flying bomb, still with its engine running, fell on the track and formed a 10ft crater. The station buildings were severely damaged, as was the track and passenger subway. Unfortunately, one member of staff was killed. These photographs were taken after the second raid.

The main station building was patched up after the two air raid incidents, but spent its last years in the condition seen here. Passengers entered by way of the three arched openings in the frontage then either ascended directly to the down platform, or used the subway if they wanted a train travelling towards central London.

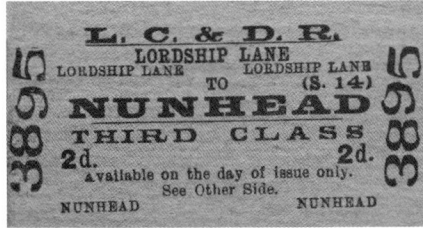 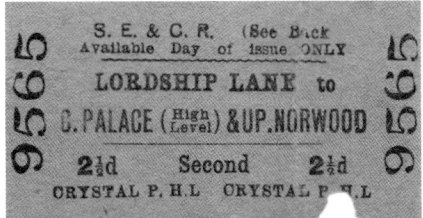 

A selection of tickets from Lordship Lane: *Left:* LCDR Third Class single to Nunhead issued 17th October, but year unclear. *Centre:* SECR Second Class single to Crystal Palace High Level issued 10th November 1906. *Right:* Southern Railway platform ticket issued 4th February 1954.

Lordship Lane – 29

LEFT: The frontage of Lordship Lane station at an unknown date, after repairs had been carried out following the enemy action of 1944.

Below: Up above, at platform level, the station latterly presented a very sparse appearance. The war damage resulted in the complete obliteration of the up side building and its replacement by temporary huts. This view, taken shortly before closure, shows the 5-04pm service from Blackfriars to Crystal Palace HL arriving at the down platform.

Above: A train for Crystal Palace HL arrives at the Lordship Lane down platform on an unknown date, just before closure. The sad remains of the main building appear on the right, whilst the temporary up side huts, erected following bomb damage, can be seen on the left.

Below: The bare empty platforms at Lordship Lane, looking towards Crystal Palace HL around 1954.

Lordship Lane station seen from its southern end around the time of closure, with the signal box in the foreground, along with the concrete platform extensions added in connection with the electrification of 1925.

A 4-SUB unit is seen leaving Lordship Lane for Crystal Palace HL in 1954. The photograph was taken from the Cox's Walk footbridge.

A 4-SUB unit is pictured passing beneath the Cox's Walk footbridge, shortly after leaving Lordship Lane station. This wooden bridge still survived in 2020 and remained very much in use. Part of the formation between here and Crescent Wood Tunnel is now a public footpath, although the section beneath and around the bridge is very overgrown.

Lordship Lane looking towards Nunhead after closure. The conductor rails had been lifted and the platform lamps removed, but it is unclear whether the main building was still standing at the time.

The main building at Lordship Lane succumbs to demolition on 3rd March 1957. To the left can be seen the former passenger subway, whilst on the right, a sign states that the nearest open station, Forest Hill, is just a five minute walk away.

Another view looking towards Nunhead, but this time taken after demolition work had started in earnest. Unfortunately the original print is not dated, but the desolate scene was probably recorded during 1957.

Upper Sydenham

Opened (London Chatham & Dover Railway): 1.8.1884.
Temporarily Closed (South Eastern & Chatham Railway): 1.1.1917 - 1. 3.1919.
and 22.5.1944 - 4.3.1946 (Southern Railway).
Closed (British Railways, Southern Region): 20.9.1954

An undated view of Upper Sydenham, looking towards the south portal of Crescent Wood Tunnel and Nunhead in pre-grouping days. The toilet blocks on the platforms were built of brick, but the adjoining shelters were largely wooden. The rear of the station house can be seen above the down side shelter.

The final station to be constructed on the Crystal Palace High Level line, Upper Sydenham was positioned between Lordship Lane and the branch terminus. It stood on a gradient of 1 in 78 and had its entrance on the south side of Wells Park Road. The station house was set back slightly from the road and from here, steps descended towards a footbridge which provided access to the two platforms. According to the Board of Trade inspection report of 29th July 1884, these were *"about 145 yards long and 2ft 9ins high."* The inspecting officer, Colonel Yolland, stated that *"The Station buildings are not yet complete and a clock has yet to be placed in the signal box. Otherwise I recommend to the Board of Trade to sanction the use of the Wells Road (Sydenham) Station* (sic) *for working the traffic."* He also requested that the Company should provide a pair of catch points on the down line *"a full train's length north of the south end of the down platform."* The Colonel's use of the name *'Wells Road'* is interesting, but when the station opened three days later, it carried the title Upper Sydenham.

Its platforms lay within a deep cutting, in a rural setting known as Hollow Coombe. Immediately to their north was the 400yd Crescent Wood Tunnel, whilst to the south the tracks were engulfed in the 439yd Paxton Tunnel. This took its name from the architect Joseph Paxton who was responsible for designing the Crystal Palace itself.

A signal box was provided at the southern end of the down platform, and this contained levers to work the home and starting signals, but not pointwork, as there was no station crossover.

Unfortunately, traffic was always fairly light, and by 1910, thirty up trains and twenty down passed through without stopping.

The signal box was closed on 4th April 1924 and demolished to allow platform lengthening in readiness for electrification. A sub-station was constructed nearby, which included a shaft taking power cables into Penge Tunnel directly underneath. The combined cost of this and the platform alterations came to £1,000, and technically made Upper Sydenham the most expensive station on the line to modernise.

Sadly, the new electric trains, which provided a full public service from 12th July 1925, failed to attract the hoped-for increase in revenue. During a census held on a day in February 1926, it was revealed that only 211 passengers departed from Upper Sydenham and 216 arrived.

During the Second World War, a great deal of rubble cleared from inner-London bombsites was dumped around the cutting behind the up platform. There was no passenger service on the branch, reputedly because of manpower shortages, between May 1944 and March 1946, but during that year, heavy rain made the accumulated debris unstable. This eventually resulted in an earthslip which occurred during May, when accumulated spoil cascaded onto the station, demolishing the up side shelter and buckling the platform fence. Single line working had to be introduced, but although operations eventually returned to normal, the shelter was never replaced.

Branch services ceased after traffic on Saturday 18th September 1954, although *'The Palace Centenarian'* steam hauled special ran the following day. This called at Lordship Lane and Honor Oak, but by-passed Upper Sydenham in both directions.

For a while after closure, the station remained more or less intact. By the second half of the decade however, the surviving shelter and the footbridge had gone, leaving just the two overgrown platforms and the house at street level. The cutting was subsequently filled in and landscaped, presumably burying the platforms in the process, but the house was retained as a private residence.

Right: Extract from the 1893-4 edition of the 1:2500 Ordnance Survey map showing the Crystal Palace High Level branch in the vicinity of Upper Sydenham station. Wells Park Road appears at the top, with the station house shown to its south. From here, a pathway led to the footbridge, which in turn provided access to the platforms. The south portal of Crescent Wood Tunnel appears immediately north of the station, whilst near the base of the extract the line can be seen disappearing into Paxton Tunnel.

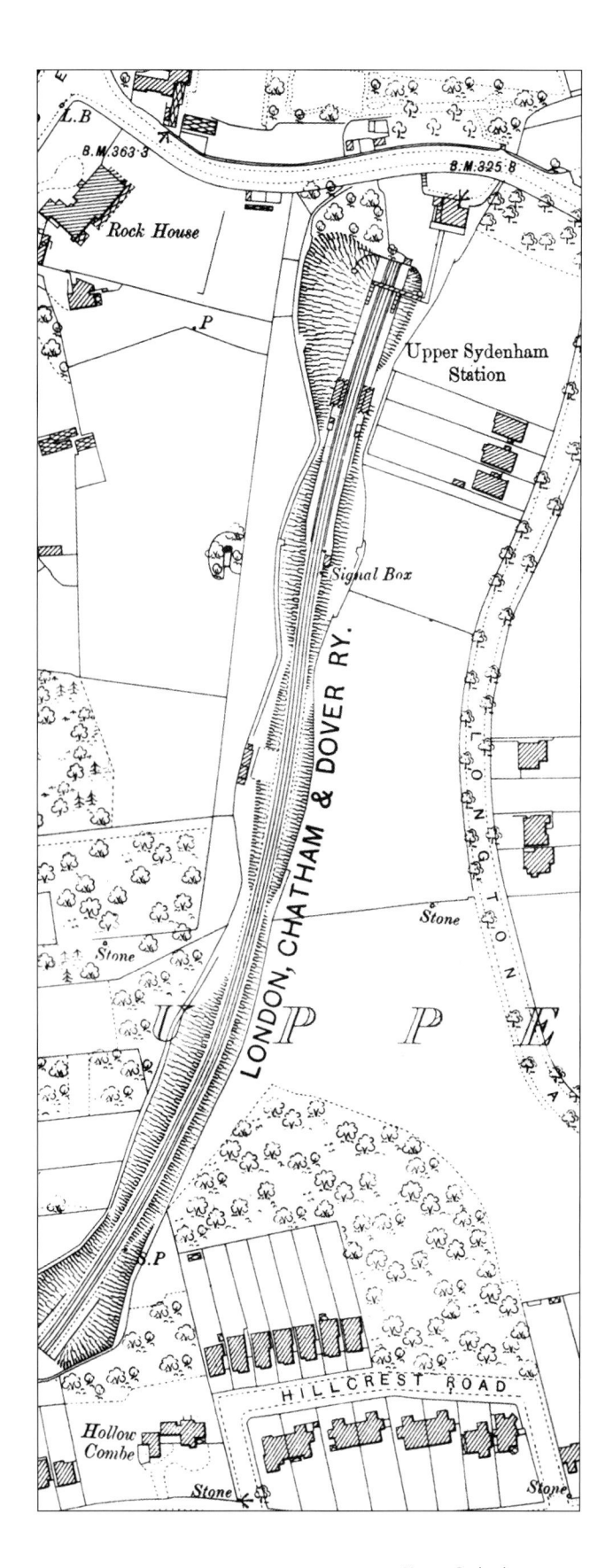

Above: Upper Sydenham station viewed from its southern end during the pre-grouping era. The curve of the formation at this point meant that the down starting signal had to be located on the up side, so that it could be more easily seen by drivers of incoming trains. The amount of ivy around the windows of the box seen on the right may have added a degree of quaint rural charm, but it must surely have restricted the signalman's field of vision!

Left: Another pre-grouping view, but this time looking in the opposite direction. It is interesting insomuch as it is the only view known to the author which shows the rear of the down side platform buildings.

Two views of the station house, set back from the south side of Wells Park Road, as it appeared in the early 1950s.

Left: To the right of the station house, stairs descended to the booking office and ultimately a footbridge which provided access to both platforms. The photograph reproduced here is thought to date from around 1945.

Below: A train bound for central London is viewed from the footbridge as it arrives at Upper Sydenham in the 1930s. One of the Crystal Palace water towers can be seen in the distance.

38 – London's Disused Railway Stations – Outer South East London

Following the onset of the Blitz, lorry loads of bomb rubble was transported to the area and deposited on land adjoining Longton Avenue. Eventually the pile, which had grown to a height of 100 feet, became unstable and it slid down the cutting side in 1946, damaging the up platform and its wooden building. Repairs were quickly carried out, but the building was never replaced. These two views were taken after the debris had been cleared away. Upper Sydenham, along with Honor Oak, retained white striping on its buildings to make them more visible to passengers in the wartime blackout.

Upper Sydenham – 39

Above: This view looks towards Nunhead and includes the up side toilet block, which survived the landslip.

Left: Unit 4678 departs from Upper Sydenham on an up service. It seems that the lettering on the running-in boards had been removed during the 'Phoney War' period and later replaced by new signs as seen on the left.

40 – London's Disused Railway Stations – Outer South East London

Above: Upper Sydenham station during demolition. The original print is undated, but it is thought that the photograph was taken around 1957.

Right: The site of Upper Sydenham station looking towards Nunhead in October 1965. Part of the up platform is vaguely visible beneath the grass on the left, whilst the top of Crescent Wood tunnel can just be seen above the foliage to the right of centre.

Upper Sydenham – 41

Crystal Palace High Level

Opened as Crystal Palace
(Crystal Palace & South London Junction Railway / London Chatham & Dover Railway): 1.8.1865.
Renamed Crystal Palace (High Level) & Upper Norwood (LCDR): 1.11.1898 although 'High Level' not always used.
Suffix '& Upper Norwood' dropped (Southern Railway): c.1923
Temporarily Closed (South Eastern & Chatham Railway): 1.1.1917 -1. 3.1919.
and 22.5.1944 - 4.3.1946 (Southern Railway).
Closed (British Railways Southern Region): 20.9.1954

Charles Barry's imposing Crystal Palace terminus, as seen from its northern end in the pre-grouping era, with SECR Class A1 0-4-4T no 625 on the left, awaiting to depart with a train for Victoria.

Designed by Charles Barry and built by the firm of Messrs. Lucas for around £100,000, Crystal Palace High Level was doubtlessly London's most grandiose branch terminus.

It owed its origins to the Crystal Palace & South London Junction Railway, which promoted a new line between Peckham and the popular south London tourist attraction on Sydenham Hill. The 'Palace' itself, designed by Sir Joseph Paxton, was originally erected in Hyde Park to house the Great Exhibition of 1851, but was only intended to be temporary. However, it met with such public acclaim, that various proposals were put forward, whereby it would be retained. Eventually however, the building was purchased, dismantled and re-erected away from the centre of town. The first pillar on the new site was driven in by Mr Samuel Laing MP on 5th August 1852 and within two years the imposing glass and iron structure was ready for its royal opening by HM Queen Victoria on 10th June 1854.

A station had been provided from the outset by the West End of London & Crystal Palace Railway, but the CP&SLJR venture would offer an alternative route.

It was always intended that the company would work in conjunction with the London Chatham & Dover Railway, although it was an independent concern with its own chairman and engineer. In June 1862, the two companies formalised the following agreement: *"That the CP&SLJR complete the line with stations, telegraphs etc and maintain it for twelve months to the satisfaction of the LCDR. The LCDR to work the line from the date of completion, paying rates and all other charges except those of direction and office and to maintain the way and works after 12 months. The receipts from traffic booked from any station on the Metropolitan Extension lines of the LCDR to stations on the Crystal Palace line and vice versa and the receipts from traffic earned locally upon the Crystal Palace line will form the gross receipts from which the working expenses of the LCDR will be deducted to the extent of not less than 50% and not more than 60%. The surplus receipts will be paid to the Crystal Palace line until they reach 4½% on the capital not to exceed £900,000 after which any excess will be divided in equal proportions between the companies."*

Messrs Peto & Betts were awarded the contract for the construction of the line and by November 1862, the CP&SLJR solicitors were authorised to acquire the necessary land.

The branch was built under the supervision of the railway's engineer, Mr F.F. Turner and involved two tunnels near its country end. That closest to the terminus stretched for a length of 439yds and was named after Paxton, as it passed near 'Rock Hill', a residence inhabited by the architect, who had personally supervised the reconstruction of his masterpiece nearby.

In August 1863, Turner informed the CP&SLJR directors that work was progressing well and anticipated that the line should be ready for opening in July 1865. Unfortunately, the task of tunnelling was subsequently delayed by winter conditions, and despite earlier confidence had only been half completed by February 1864. This in turn delayed a start being made on the Crystal Palace station, as spoil removal had to wait until the tunnels had been finished.

Right: The station as shown on the 1:2500 Ordnance Survey map of 1894, with part of the Crystal Palace seen to its right. On the opposite side of the formation were sidings which served the coal yard and were also used for stock storage. These were accessed by means of a long headshunt, which stretched behind the western wall of the trainshed. Near the north end of this was a footbridge which connected the station with Farquhar Road, although this was removed sometime before the branch closed. To the right of the siding stop blocks, the running lines can be seen disappearing into the south portal of Paxton Tunnel.

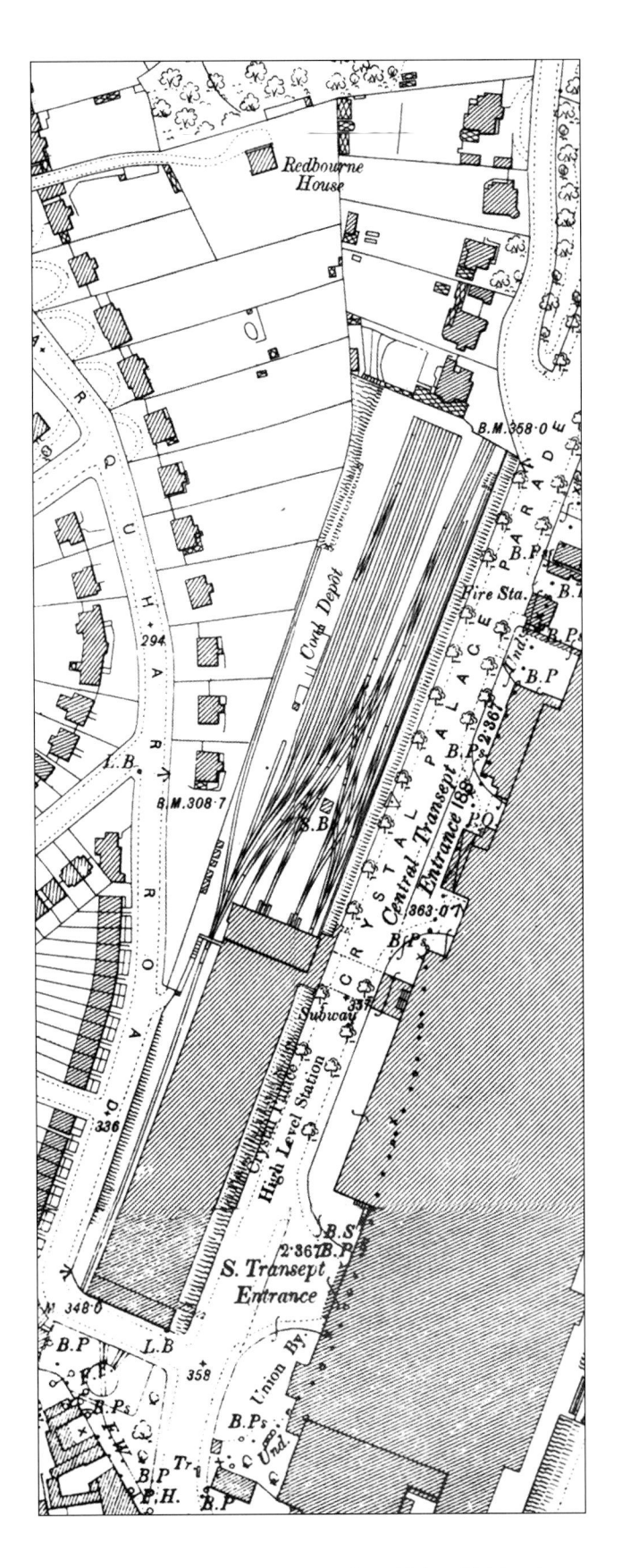

Crystal Palace High Level – 43

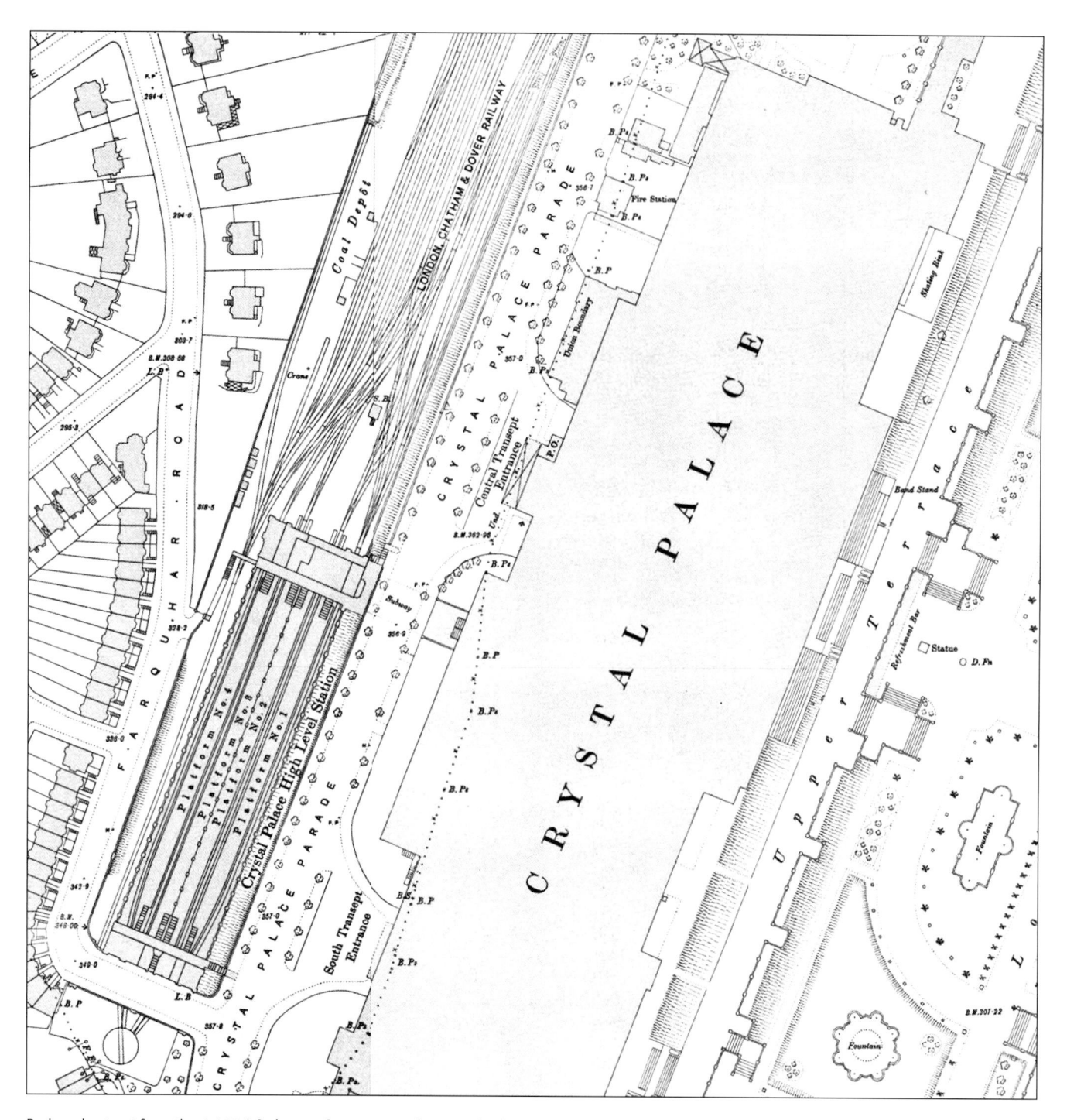

Reduced extract from the 1:1056 Ordnance Survey map of 1895, which shows the internal arrangements of the station, with its four platforms. A Southern Railway diagram of 1945 stated that these had the following lengths: Platform 1 - 450ft, Platform 2 - 510ft, Platform 3 - 535ft and Platform 4 - 428ft.

The main station entrance was at its southern end, on the north side of Farquhar Road, but access was also available around the corner in Crystal Palace Parade. A further booking office was provided at the north end and this was linked by means of a subway with the Palace itself. In September 1865, the Illustrated London News stated that *"...the passengers will have easy access by a handsome and well lighted subway 40ft wide, ascending to the main floor either of the centre transept or behind the concert room, by a broad flight of steps... the distance from the station to the central transept is only 30 yards..."* These facilities were for the use of first class passengers only, whilst second and third class passengers used the main entrance. Immediately south of the station, on the opposite side of Farquhar Road can be seen the locomotive turntable.

Once this had been achieved, however, construction continued apace and in June 1865, the date originally estimated for completion, the company was confident enough to apply for the line's Board of Trade inspection.

Captain Rich made two consecutive visits and his report dated 29th June observed that the *"New line commences at a bridge over Gordon Road."* It was double track throughout and there were stations at both Lordship Lane and Crystal Palace. He described the gradients as *"generally 1 in 80 or 1 in 78 with short pieces at 1 in 300 for present and contemplated stations"*. Unfortunately, the company were clearly premature in requesting the inspection, as the report stated that the stations were *"both incomplete as regards the buildings, the platforms, safe access to the platforms and they require clocks .... A turntable is being built at the Palace and is nearly complete ... With regard to the terminal station at the Palace (which consists of two long arched covered ways, fronted with the station building) I cannot express an opinion in its present state. The iron and glass roof over one section is nearly completed, but none of the scaffolding used in erecting it is taken down. The platform is crowded with scaffolding under the station building and several scaffold poles are erected at other parts. The station building, under which the two lines now proposed to open pass, to the platforms is unfinished, and the whole front is covered with scaffolding on which men were working. The signal arrangements provided to work the two lines is quite insufficient for the station when complete, a temporary staircase and temporary passage which form access to the station are quite unsuited and unsafe for a Crystal Palace traffic."* With so little actually completed, it must have come as no surprise when Captain Rich refused to sanction the line's opening!

He returned a month later and reported on 20th July that *"Work has been done except Lordship Lane and the larger half of Crystal Palace Station ... The Company do not intend to use Lordship Lane or the incompleted portion of the Crystal Palace Station at present."*

Permission to open the branch was duly received and trains began operating on 1st August 1865. These ran from Victoria and left the London, Brighton & South Coast Railway 18ch east of Peckham Rye. The boundary between the two companies was known as Cow Lane Junction. They then climbed towards the Palace, but until 1st September 1865, when Lordship Lane opened, there were no intermediate stations.

As is apparent from Captain Rich's report, the Crystal Palace terminus was still unfinished at its time of opening, so only half of it was in use. One of the features which awaited completion was a 40ft wide Byzantine-styled subway, which was to give First Class passengers direct access from the northern end of the station into the Palace's central transept. No expense was spared on its construction and master-craftsmen were brought over from Italy specifically for the task.

The north end of the station seen at an unknown date around the late nineteenth century, with its Saxby & Farmer signal box in the foreground. To the extreme right can be seen part of the footbridge which crossed above the headshunt to the west of the trainshed and provided an additional link between the station and Farquhar Road.

Crystal Palace High Level – 45

Eventually the work was completed and as the scaffolding was removed, the impressive structure could at last be fully appreciated. It was constructed in red and yellow brick and had towers positioned at each of its four corners. From the tops of these rose a succession of square turrets, with pinnacled roofs, which created extra height and added an air of distinction.

At its southern end, the frontage faced onto Farquhar Road and included a doorway which provided access. From here, passengers entered a short passageway, then descended a flight of around eleven stairs to reach the various station facilities and offices. To the right lay a refreshment room, the booking hall and ladies, whilst to the left could be found the gents and a Third Class dining room. The central steps also led onto a gallery, which in addition to acting as a footbridge above the tracks below, also served a small side entrance which stood on Crystal Palace Parade. This was linked to the gallery by means of a stairway and proved popular with those visiting the South Transept of the 'Palace', which was located on the opposite side of the road.

Similar facilities were provided at the north end, but here they were intended for First Class passengers and were therefore more spaciously laid out. Steps again descended from Crystal Palace Parade, but there was also the subway which led beneath the main road into the Central Transept. Directly facing this was a booking office, and access to a further gallery, similar to that serving the southern entrance. Immediately after turning into this, passengers would encounter a restaurant to their right, followed by a gents, a general waiting room and a ladies. There was also a connecting footbridge to Farquhar Road, which curved round and followed the station's western boundary.

There were four wooden platforms, of which the outer pair were islands. The other two lay in the centre and

46 – London's Disused Railway Stations – Outer South East London

Facing page: The doorway in the centre of the frontage onto Farquhar Road was originally the chief means of access but latterly it seems that all passengers used the smaller entrance in Crystal Palace Parade. This is the imposing frontage onto Farquhar Road with the entrance at centre. A newspaper report, subsequently copied by the *Illustrated London News* of 30th September 1865, wrongly attributed the design of the station to Edward Barry, instead of his brother Charles. However the *ILN* of 7th October 1865 corrected this error and stated that Charles Barry *"also designed and superintended the building of the station at Lordship's Lane* (sic) *on the new line between Sydenham and Peckham"*.

Right: The Crystal Palace Parade entrance at the south end of the station, seen in 1954. This led directly into the gallery, which provided access to both the booking hall and the platforms.

although these could perhaps be regarded as forming an island, they were separated from each other by a wall of substantial brick arches. All the platforms were linked to the galleries at either end by stairways, whilst above rose two spans of glazed overall roof. These stretched the full length of the premises and were supported on their inner sides by the central dividing wall.

At the southernmost end, the tracks continued beyond the trainshed to a locomotive turntable, set within a 44ft 10in diameter well. Although from the outset, the trains were generally worked by tank locomotives, the turntable proved useful for engines running-round after arrival, as it took up less space than the pointwork which would otherwise have been necessary.

Behind the station's west-side wall lay a single track, which was provided with a loading dock and served as a headshunt for a goods and coal yard which was located to the north of the site, parallel to the approach tracks. There were also some carriage sidings on this side of the line, with a couple more, used for berthing stock, opposite them.

Initially, the service comprised nineteen non-stop trains, which ran in both directions on weekdays, but for a while there was little in the way of residential traffic. Nevertheless, within a year the daily service was increased to thirty-three return journeys, but even at this early stage, public enthusiasm for the 'Palace' was beginning to wane. The situation worsened when a fire broke out in the Northern Transept during 1866 and left it completely destroyed.

Such problems seriously blighted the finances of the CP&SLJR, which was also beginning to experience troubles with the LCDR. A lack of adequate signalling at the terminus resulted in the larger company threatening to withdraw its operation of the line and this situation was subsequently exacerbated by various other disagreements.

Meanwhile, the LCDR were busy further north, by constructing the first section of branch linking the CP&SLJR at Nunhead with Greenwich. This was brought into use on 18th September 1871, seventeen days after Nunhead station was opened, 54ch east of Cow Lane Junction.

The bad atmosphere between the two companies continued and was brought to a head in 1874 when the LCDR obtained authority to build a connection onto the rival route to Crystal Palace, which dated back to 1854 and was now owned by the London Brighton & South Coast Railway. This meant that the 'Palace' could be served from both Victoria and the newly opened Holborn Viaduct, without using the CP&SLJR branch, therefore effectively leaving it without trains. The Crystal Palace & South London Junction Railway realised that it was facing an ultimatum and the Board decided to take the only viable option. They agreed to sell out to the larger organisation and their undertaking was officially absorbed into the LCDR in 1875.

By the beginning of 1877, there were twenty-four weekday trains from Victoria to Crystal Palace between 6.55am and 10.52pm, of which one ran non-stop and covered the journey in twenty-five minutes. There were also thirty trains originating from the Metropolitan Extension, with some completing the run in less than half an hour.

As time progressed, additional stations were opened on the branch, with the first at Honor Oak as early as December 1865 and the second at Upper Sydenham nineteen years later. These, together with Lordship Lane, all catered for the needs of residential traffic, but the terminus was still chiefly used by the declining number of people who wished to visit the Crystal Palace.

The station was renamed Crystal Palace (High Level) & Upper Norwood on 1st November 1898, no doubt in an attempt to drum up more use by commuters, but it wasn't a great success.

The Crystal Palace offered an excellent venue for various special events, but as the new century dawned these were becoming less and less. The FA Cup Final was held in the grounds from 1894 until 1914 and The Festival of Empire and Imperial Exhibition of 1911 also proved very popular. At times like this, the ample station came into its own, and the line proved its worth. During the 1911 Show, which ran between March and October, trains formed of ten four-wheel coaches covered the distance between Victoria and Crystal Palace in a quarter of an hour, which was two minutes faster than the newly electrified LBSCR route linking the same points. On one day of the event, a special fete was held in connection with the coronation of King George V, which required the operation of forty-seven special trains, full of school children, in and out of Crystal Palace (High Level). To cope with this influx, ninety extra staff were brought in to work at the terminus and sixty-one out of the regular ninety-eight services had to be cancelled to provide the pathways.

In 1914, the 'Palace' itself was taken over by the Admiralty to be used as a recruiting and training centre. By this time, the residential traffic, which previously had used the stations at Honor Oak and Lordship Lane, had been eroded by tramway competition, so the branch seemed an ideal candidate for wartime economies.

The services over the Metropolitan Extension into Moorgate Street were reduced in January 1915 and ceased completely in April of the following year. This left just the Victoria trains, which soldiered on until the beginning of 1917, when they were suspended for the duration. For a time, steam railcars, redundant from elsewhere, were worked down the branch and placed into storage outside the station.

The branch eventually re-opened on 1st March 1919, but the service only operated to and from St Paul's and Ludgate Hill, as both the Moorgate Street and Victoria trains had been withdrawn for good.

A proposal to electrify the line was made in 1920, but nothing happened until after it became part of the Southern Railway three years later. Conductor rails were subsequently laid and electric multiple-units began operating for staff training purposes between Nunhead and Crystal Palace on 1st April 1925. The full public service over the line was introduced three months later on 12th July, with trains every twenty minutes on weekdays, and every half-hour on Sunday. These ran to and from St. Paul's, which was renamed Blackfriars in 1937, and completed the journey in twenty-five minutes, having called at all intermediate stations.

The Crystal Palace High Level locomotive turntable, separated from the station by the bridge carrying Farquhar Road.

Unfortunately, electrification did not bring the up-turn in traffic receipts that the Southern Railway had hoped for. During a traffic survey held during February 1926, it was found that each train left the terminus carrying an average of just thirteen passengers and the numbers at Upper Sydenham were also very disappointing. Therefore from 19th July 1926, the service was reduced to half hourly on Saturday afternoons after 3pm, although no other changes were deemed necessary.

On the night of 30th November 1936, a fire broke out near the Egyptian Room in the 'Palace' and within thirty minutes, the great glass building was engulfed in flames from end to end. It was the most spectacular conflagration in Britain for many years and the glow in the sky could be clearly seen for many miles around. People turned-out in crowds to witness the spectacle and numbers of these climbed onto the roofs of old LCDR six-wheeled coaches which were stored near the High Level station. Although only separated from the fire by the width of Crystal Palace Parade, the old terminus remained unscathed and when all the excitement was over, the Southern Railway laid on a special train to take many of the spectators home.

Ninety fire engines and five hundred firemen were engaged in fighting the blaze, but they were unable to save most of the structure, which dissolved into a huge molten mass in the ferocious heat. All that remained standing were a pair of 284ft high towers and a few ruined footings. With the 'Palace' died any hope of a revival to the High Level station and it fell into a period of terminal decline, with matters worsened by the onset of war in 1939.

From 1st January 1940, the Sunday and off-peak weekdays services were reduced to hourly, which was understandable, but more drastic cuts were to follow. Through workings to and from central London were withdrawn after 6th January 1941 and replaced by a shuttle from Nunhead, which connected with Catford Loop Line trains. This arrangement lasted until 21st May 1944, when, in the interests of economy, the branch passenger service was suspended completely.

Nearly two months later, on 13th July, a bridge at Cow Lane was hit by a V1 flying bomb and destroyed. A temporary replacement was soon installed by the Royal Engineers and traffic was able to be reinstated in just ten days. Although the line had been closed to public services, the sidings at Crystal Palace (High Level) were used for stock storage and contained a number of Pullman cars, which were surplus to needs due to wartime circumstances. At the same time, 5-BEL Pullman unit No 3052 which had been damaged by enemy action outside Victoria, was stored beneath the overall roof. The High Level station survived the raids largely unscathed, although the pounding of nearby anti-aircraft guns destroyed some of its glazing.

The branch shuttles linking Crystal Palace with Nunhead were restored on 4th March 1946, with rush-hour Blackfriars through trains following five months later on 11th August. A full service, running at half-hourly intervals, and supplemented with additionals during the peaks, was introduced from 27th September 1948, but the Sunday workings failed to return.

By now, the years of neglect were seriously beginning to show and the once-fine terminus took on an air of desolation. The entrance and facilities at its northern end had fallen into disuse and rain falling through the broken glass overall roof stimulated the growth of foliage around the tracks. Ferns sprung up through the rotting wooden platforms, whilst above them, nets were hung to protect passengers from falling debris. Not that there were many passengers to protect, as their numbers had been far out-weighed by the rats which now scurried around the place completely unheeded.

Plans to close the branch were announced at the beginning of 1954 and implemented in the autumn. The regular service was withdrawn after Saturday 18th September, but a final steam-hauled special was operated the following day. Named *The Palace Centenarian*, in recognition of the 'Palace' being opened a hundred years earlier, it was worked by ex-SECR C class 0-6-0s. It was booked to depart from the High Level at 2.22pm, then run to Richmond for a 3.19pm arrival. After a break of nearly one and a half hours, it left at 4.48pm, then travelled by way of Kingston, Wimbledon and East Putney to Clapham Junction, where a pilot loco was coupled ahead of the train engine. It then continued through Herne Hill and Tulse Hill to the former LBSCR station at Crystal Palace Low Level, where a one minute stop was scheduled. From here the special, which was formed of pre-war stock and included a buffet car, headed past Sydenham and London Bridge to Blackfriars where it reversed. The two locos at the front were detached and replaced by a fresh pair from the same class. From Blackfriars, the train made a direct run back to the High Level, where it was due to terminate at 7.10pm. En-route it called at Lordship Lane and Honor Oak in both directions and tickets were issued carrying the heading '*Special Last Steam Train On The Crystal Palace High Level Branch*'.

Considering how little the line had been used in later years, it certainly proved popular on its final day and crowds of on-lookers watched the last train go by. It had been financed by Mr G.R. Lockie, who lived locally and organised many 'ramblers' excursions' during the 1950s. All places had been sold prior to the event, no doubt because the closure of an electrified branch line in London was very unusual. The weather was fine and ideal for photography, so fortunately the event was well recorded. The power for the third-rail had been cut off the previous night, and a number of people took advantage of this by straying onto the track, particularly at Crystal Palace High Level. Detonators were laid at various locations along the branch, and there was a great deal of whistling from the locomotives, as their drivers acknowledged waves from the lineside throng.

On arrival at the branch terminus, the two locomotives made their way individually to the turntable and, having turned, hauled the empty stock back to Stewarts Lane depot.

After closure, the process of decay continued, but the building remained standing, despite the removal of the branch tracks during 1956 and 1957.

During 1957, the well-known film producer, Ken Russell included the derelict terminus in a short production entitled *Amelia and The Angel*. The station interior featured prominently in some of the shots and, in addition to having a charming story line, the film provides a good record of its condition at the time.

In the end, the station succumbed to the inevitable and demolition took place in April 1961. After this, the site lay empty, but it has since been used for housing.

The brick retaining wall survives along the west side of Crystal Palace Parade, together with the subway which once connected the station with the 'Palace' itself. With octagonal stone columns supporting red and white brickwork vaulting, it provides a reminder of the grandeur that once was the old High Level terminus. The subway now has Listed status, but is normally not available for public viewing. Much easier to see are two bricked-up openings on the west side of Crystal Palace Parade, which were once part of the entrances leading into the north and south station footbridges.

To the north of the site, beyond the erstwhile expanse of sidings, the southern portal of Paxton Tunnel remains as another obvious relic of the line, but the days when trains pulled up the gradients to Crystal Palace (High Level) are now long gone.

Looking north from Crystal Palace High Level on 3rd October 1953, with the 69-lever signal box to the left and the southern portal of Paxton Tunnel on the right. Behind the box can be seen the sidings which served the coal yard.

50 – London's Disused Railway Stations – Outer South East London

The Palace Centenarian special was promoted in the railway press of September 1954 and interested readers were invited to contact the organiser for tickets. The train was expected to leave Crystal Palace High Level *"at about 2pm"* and travel by way of the Metropolitan Widened Lines to the then recently closed branch linking Finsbury Park with Alexandra Palace. Here it would reverse then return by way of Canonbury, Willesden Junction, Kew Bridge, Clapham Junction, Tulse Hill, Crystal Palace Low Level, London Bridge and Blackfriars, but this was not to be. A letter was written by Mr Lockie and sent to all applicants, explaining why the route had to be changed.

Below: Ex-SECR Class C 0-6-0 No 31576, sporting a wreath on her smokebox door and two large headboards, is prepared for departure from Crystal Palace High Level and starts its journey.

36, Harold Road,
Upper Norwood,
London, S.E.19.

4th September, 1954.

Thank you for your enquiry regarding the Special Commemorative Train from Crystal Palace (High Level) on Sunday, 19th September.

Since the notification appeared in the September issues of the "Railway World" and "Railway Magazine", it has unfortunately been necessary to make considerable alterations to the proposed route because of Engineers Possession of the track between Faringdon and Kings Cross over which our Special would have required to pass. I was not informed about this until very recently.

The route will, therefore, now be as follows:-

Crystal Palace (H.L.) - Nunhead - Factory Junction - Clapham Junction - Richmond. There will be a stopover of 1½ hours at this point, after which the train will continue via Kingston - Wimbledon - East Putney - Clapham Jct. - Factory Jct. - Herne Hill - Tulse Hill - West Norwood - Crystal Palace (L.L.) - Forest Hill - London Bridge (H.L.) - Metropolitan Jct - Blackfriars, where the train will reverse on the bridge and return to Crystal Palace (H.L.).

It is not possible to run this train purely for railway enthusiasts at such short notice, in fact it has mainly been promoted to give residents and former users along the Crystal Palace (H.L.) Nunhead line a farewell commemorative half-days outing and a considerable response from such people is expected.

The train will be steam-hauled throughout and a Refreshment or Cafeteria car will be supplied. An ex L.B.S.C. C2X goods engine should haul the train as far as Blackfriars Bridge and an ex S.E. & C.R. engine for the final stage back to Crystal Palace (H.L.)

Train Times are as under:-

CRYSTAL PALACE (H.L.)	2.22 p.m.	dep.
Lordship Lane	2.27 "	"
Honor Oak	2.32 "	"
Peckham Rye	2.41 "	"
Richmond	3.19 "	arr.
Richmond	4.48 "	dep.
CRYSTAL PALACE (L.L.)	6.04 "	arr.
"	6.05 "	dep.
Elephant & Castle	6.38 "	arr.
Peckham Rye	6.50 "	"
Honor Oak	6.59 "	"
Lordship Lane	7.04 "	"
CRYSTAL PALACE (H.L.)	7.10 "	"

The overall fare will be 6/-d (children under 14 half price if accompanied by adult) entitling ticket holders to board or alight at any intermediate station on line of route. I am informed that if it had been possible to complete the tour to Alexandra Palace as originally planned, the cost would have been about 15/- because of extra expense.

TICKETS and handbill with further information will be available after September 5th from myself at the above address.

Applicants are requested to enclose an addressed envelope with appropriate remittance, also to indicate, if possible, at which station they intend to join and leave the train. Certain stops have been put in for the convenience of those who may not be able to complete the entire tour.

This will almost certainly be the last passenger train to ever traverse the Crystal Palace (H.L.) - Nunhead line and it is doubtful if there has been any instance of steam haulage of passengers over it since the 1925 electrification. The motive power is unusual, and most of the remainder of the route cannot be traversed by steam in the ordinary way, lastly the fare is reasonable considering the special arrangements necessary.

Accomodation on this train is limited, hence early application is advised.

G. B. Lockie
ORGANISER.

P.S. I shall be pleased to book you for two seats on receipt of remittance. GBL.

Above: The south end gallery, viewed at an unknown date, possibly soon after closure. The doorway at the far end led to the entrance in Crystal Palace Parade, close to the junction with Farquhar Road.

Left: The south end of the station around 1956, looking towards the bridge carrying Farquhar Road.

Right: The north end gallery lying derelict in the second half of the 1950s. The doorway at the end served the former passenger footbridge which spanned the headshunt and led to Farquhar Road.

Below: The north end of Crystal Palace High Level station, taken from the westernmost island platform at an unknown date before track lifting had been completed. By the early 1950s, the fine terminus had fallen into disrepair and rats could frequently be heard disturbing the silence as they scurried beneath the wooden platforms. After closure it became progressively derelict and parts of it, such as the footbridge seen here, started to collapse.

Crystal Palace High Level – 53

Above: The north end of the station, possibly around 1956-7, seen from the easternmost platform.

Left: Looking south along the eastern side, after the electric conductor rails had been lifted, but whilst some track was still in place. The central dividing wall with its open arches can be seen on the right.

54 – London's Disused Railway Stations – Outer South East London

Externally, Charles Barry's building looked impressive to the last, even with its approach tracks disappearing under foliage and the signal box boarded-up. This photograph dates from 1956 and was taken from the site of the former goods yard.

Ex-LBSCR Class C2X 0-6-0 No 32553 is seen on an engineers' train at Crystal Palace High Level during the early stages of track lifting in 1956.

Above: The east side of the station, as seen from the the north end gallery after the track had been lifted.

Left: Another view taken from the north end gallery, but this time showing the station's west side.

Above: The southern portal of Paxton Tunnel seen in 1966, with the cutting retaining wall partly hidden by foliage on the right.

Right: A section of the cutting retaining wall to the west of Crystal Palace Parade as it appeared in July 2017.

Crystal Palace High Level – 57

From the 'Palace', passengers holding first class rail tickets could descend to a roofed concourse, then walk through the subway which led them to the north end of the station. The upper view shows the east side of the concourse, whilst that below shows the west, with a glimpse of the vaulted subway through the arched openings.
Both photographs were taken in January 1987 and show evidence of the erstwhile roof, which was removed many years ago.

58 – London's Disused Railway Stations – Outer South East London

The splendid subway beneath Crystal Palace Parade, which once linked the High Level station with the Palace itself.

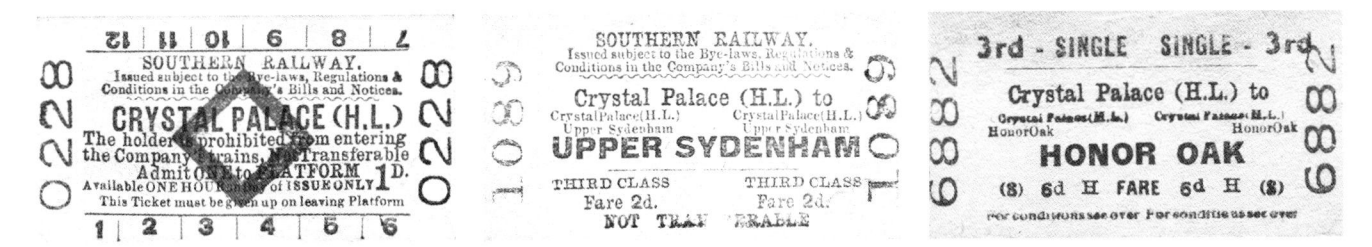

A further selection of Crystal Palace High Level tickets: *Left* Southern Railway platform ticket issued 30th April 1954. *Centre* Southern Railway Third Class single to Upper Sydenham issued 4th May 1949. *Right* British Railways Third Class single to Honor Oak issued 18th September 1954, the last day of regular passenger services.

Penge

Opened (West End of London & Crystal Palace Railway): 3.5.1858 (possibly).
Closed (London Chatham & Dover Railway): c1860 (possibly).
Also referred to as 'Beckenham Road'. Shown after closure on LCDR deposited plans of November 1873 as 'Penge Lane'.

The short-lived Penge station of the West End of London & Crystal Palace Railway was located on the Norwood - Bromley line, which was authorised in 1854.

The route had originally been intended to continue to Farnborough, but it was cut back to Bromley before construction started three years later. At a committee meeting held on 20th January 1858, the WELCPR discussed the proposed stations, and accepted a revised scheme from the engineer, John Fowler, which reduced the original estimate by £1,000. The minutes recorded that *"it was resolved that the stations at Shortlands and Penge Road be constructed according to the plans now submitted by the Engineer"*, and work was put into hand.

Although referred to as 'Penge Road', the station was actually situated to the north of what is now Beckenham Road and was then surrounded by fields. Nevertheless, the eastern edge of urban Penge was about 300yds away and the premises were reasonably convenient for those living in the western fringes of Beckenham.

The line was inspected on behalf of the Board of Trade by Lieutenant-Colonel Yolland and his report of 28th April 1858 stated: *"I have this day inspected that portion of the West End of London and Crystal Palace Railway situated between the Bridge on the - Down Line over the Brighton Railway at Norwood and its junction with the Mid Kent Railway near Beckenham Station which portion is double throughout, and from Beckenham Station to Shortlands Station near Bromley which is only laid at the present time as a single line, but the land has been purchased and the works are constructed for a double line ... Stations have been constructed at Penge and Shortlands ... In making my inspection I noticed the following:- 1st. Clocks are required at Penge and Shortlands Stations. 2nd. The Handles of the distant Signals to be brought together at Penge."*

Lt. Col. Yolland also required ramps to be added to the platforms at Penge and other changes to be made along the route. The various alterations were undertaken and traffic commenced with a Crystal Palace - Bromley shuttle service on 3rd May 1858. Later in the month the Company Secretary reported various arrangements which had been made in connection with the opening. These included the appointment of a stationmaster and porter at Penge, whose weekly wages amounted to twenty-five shillings and sixteen shillings respectively. However, what happened next is uncertain.

Lt. Col. Yolland's improvements had presumably been completed and the necessary staff had been employed, but from then on there is no further mention of Penge station in the minute books. The mystery deepens as it did not appear in Bradshaw, therefore suggesting that there had been some last minute change of mind and opening had been postponed indefinitely. The Company Secretary's minutes regarding staffing were written on 14th May 1858, eleven days after the line opened and Penge is just one of the stations listed, with no suggestion that its circumstances were different in any way. Therefore it is perhaps possible that the station was brought into use, but not advertised.

Unlike the rest of the WELCPR system, the LBSCR had declined to work the 'Extension Line' and it was eventually sold to the London Chatham & Dover Railway in 1859. On 3rd December 1860, the Crystal Palace - Bromley shuttles were replaced by through trains to and from Victoria and the station at Penge possibly ceased to function at the same time, if indeed it had opened in the first place.

With such little recorded information it is tempting to accept that the station was never brought into use, but two published local histories of the area suggest otherwise. Robert Borrowman writing in *Beckenham Past and Present* in 1910 stated that *"There was for many years a station on the latter system where the line crosses the Beckenham Road"*, although its physical existence does not necessarily imply that it was ever used. The written recollections of a certain Walter Mathew of Copers Cope Farm however, include reference to a German-born resident of Beckenham High Street who was the first and possibly only passenger to use the premises. The WELCPR station at Penge is therefore somewhat of an enigma and it is little wonder that H. V. Borley did not include it in his *Chronology of London Railways*.

The station house was occupied by a platelayer and his wife (after being vacated by the stationmaster) until around 1910, but the date of its demolition is not known.

In 1874, a curve, 16½ chains in length, was authorised to link the abandoned station site with the LCDR route towards Victoria. This was initially known as the Beckenham Loop, but it was renamed the Penge Loop before officially opening in July 1879. It was laid on embankment for its entire distance, although a girder bridge was erected to carry the double track formation above the east end of Barnmead Road. Although the line was indeed available for traffic, there is again doubt as to whether it was ever used. After the relevant section of LCDR Victoria main line had been quadrupled in 1886, the track was lifted, although a stretch of it was reinstated as a carriage siding in 1899. Today parts of this obscure connection remain visible, together with evidence of the bridge over Barnmead Road, but all traces of the WELCPR Penge station vanished long ago. To end on a more positive note however, part of the formation once served by the old station was incorporated into the Croydon Tramlink system and a stop, named Beckenham Road, was erected close to the former station site. This opened for public traffic on 23rd May 2000, and is served by trams travelling to and from Beckenham Junction.

Extract from the 1:2500 Ordnance Survey map of 1894 showing Penge as *"Station Disused"* near the bottom to the right. The building, along with a short length of platform, adjoined the southern junction of the Beckenham (or Penge) Loop, which was trackless at the time and was described as *"Old Railway"*. Presumably Penge station originally had two platforms, but that which served the other line must have disappeared when the loop was being constructed in the late 1870s. Kent House station, which of course remains very much in use, appears near the top of the map.

The South Eastern Railway

In February 1836, the initial section of the London & Greenwich Railway was opened between Spa Road, Bermondsey and Deptford. This was the first conventional railway to serve Greater London and it carried passengers from the beginning.

The line remained independent for nine years, but in 1845 financial pressures resulted in it being leased to the South Eastern Railway.

The first stretch of the SER was sanctioned in the previous decade, with a view to linking London with the Kent coast. Although officially titled the South Eastern Railway from the outset, it was often referred to in early days as the 'Dover Railway' or the 'London & Dover Railway'.

As the years progressed and its system grew, the SER took on the responsibility of operating services for various smaller companies such as the Mid-Kent Railway, which had opened its first section between Lewisham and Beckenham Junction in January 1857. Although its trains were always worked by the South Eastern, the little MKR remained nominally independent until the mid 1860s when it was finally absorbed by the larger organisation.

Another Greater London route in which the SER was involved was that linking Woodside and Selsdon Road. This was shared with the London Brighton & South Coast Railway and was managed under the title of the Woodside & South Croydon Joint Committee. The line, which opened in 1885, was never a financial success and was permanently closed in 1983, although part of it was later incorporated into the Croydon Tramlink system.

For many years there was a great deal of rivalry between the SER and the London Chatham & Dover Railway. The results of this were invariably detrimental to the fortunes of both companies, so they eventually agreed to amalgamate under a joint committee. The SER and LCDR officially retained their individual titles, but from 1899 their network was worked and managed as the South Eastern & Chatham Railway.

To the north-east of Coombe Road station on the Woodside & South Croydon line lay Woodside, Park Hill and Coombe Lane Tunnels, with the latter being closest to the station. Normally, one tunnel would have sufficed, but the nature of the soil meant that the central section had to be constructed using the cut and cover system. This view was taken in March 1984, after the track had been lifted and shows the joins between the three bores. This section of route now forms part of the Croydon Tramlink network.

Church Manorway Halt

Opened (South Eastern & Chatham Railway): 1.1.1917.
Closed (South Eastern & Chatham Railway): 1.1.1920.
Sometimes shown as Church Manor Way Halt or Church Manor-Way Halt.

Opened on Monday 1st January 1917 for the use of munitions workers travelling from nearby temporary accommodation to the Royal Arsenal, Church Manorway Halt was situated 71 chains east of Plumstead on the North Kent Line.

It comprised two platforms and was served by loops constructed either side of the existing tracks. Both platforms had a length of about 540ft and varied in width from 6ft at their most narrow to 9ft at their widest. They were accessed by means of pathways from the east side of Church Manorway Crossing, where a footbridge was erected in the interests of safety. A diagram published by the SECR at the time of opening shows what appears to be two small huts at the platform end of these paths, which may have held stocks of tickets, although this cannot be confirmed. Waiting shelters were provided about mid-way along the length of each platform and we know from Colonel Pringle's Board of Trade inspection report that the *"necessary fencing and lighting arrangements"* had been provided. He also stated that the name boards had *"been fixed"*, although this was perhaps to be expected as his visit took place seven months after opening!

A signal box was erected on the down side, between the rear of the waiting shelter and the platform end. Colonel Pringle went on to describe the layout: *"In addition to the facing and trailing connections leading to* (the) *loops, there are also trailing crossovers between the main lines at each end, and a new facing connection on the down main line leading to King's Norton Siding. The necessary up and down running signals, as well as those for shunting purposes have been provided.*

The points and signals are worked from a new signal-box forming an additional block post which is now known as Plumstead "C" signal box. One of the levers controls the gates of the adjoining No.4 Church Manorway Crossing, a gateman being in charge. The interlocking is correct. The down advanced signal is 616yds from the signal-box, and the track circuit work is, I think, necessary between that signal and the facing points in the rear ...

In view of the additional traffic on the main lines, it has been arranged to control the gates of an old cross crossing (sic) *(known as Bostall Manorway). A ground frame containing three levers has been provided alongside the crossing for this purpose. This ground frame is released from Abbey Wood Station signal box. The release lever interlocks with the down stop and up advanced signals on each side of the crossing. The control lever in the groundframe at the crossing backlocks the release lever in Abbey Wood signal-box.*

There is telephone communication between Abbey Wood and the level crossing. Bostall Manorway Crossing ground frame contains 3 working levers ... "

A note in the report's margin stated that Plumstead 'C' signal box contained *"45 working and spare levers"*, but a signalling diagram issued by the SECR at the time of opening indicates a total of forty-eight levers, of which three were spare.

The halt and its loops remained in use for a while after the armistice, but with the decline in munition production, it was no longer required. It was therefore closed at the beginning of 1920 and subsequently demolished.

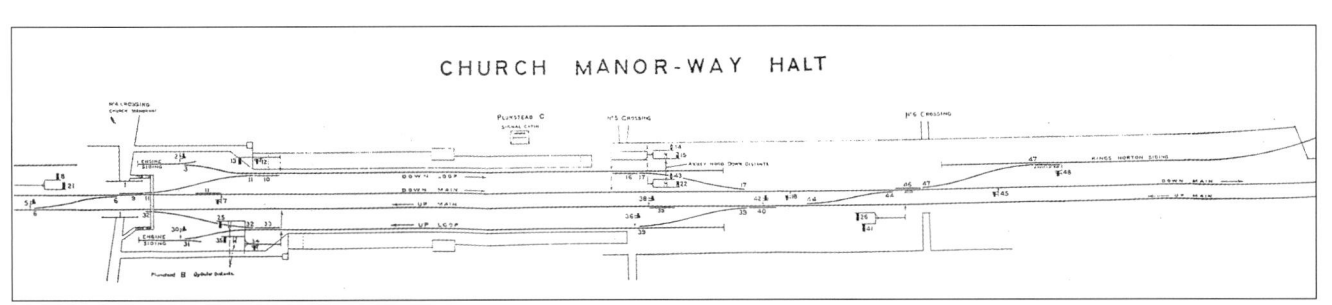

Right: Third class single ticket from Church Manorway Halt to Plumstead. The rear of the ticket is damaged, so the date of issue is unknown.

Below: Track and signalling plan of Church Manorway, as it appeared in South Eastern & Chatham Railway Permanent Way Notice No 32, which was issued to staff on 23rd December 1916 to advise them of the changes brought about in connection with the halt's opening.

Private and not for Circulation. No. 32 (P.W.)

South Eastern and Chatham
RAILWAY. (S. 11,001-H.)

> Each Station Master, and Foreman in the Engineer's and Locomotive Departments, will be held responsible that this Notice is properly and promptly distributed to all the Staff (Engine Drivers and Guards particularly) concerned; and it will likewise be the duty of the Officers and Servants at each Station (in the several Departments) to obtain or read a copy, as no excuse of want of knowledge, &c., will be admitted.

To the Officers and Servants of this and other Companies concerned.

OPENING OF NEW HALT
ALSO
NEW SIGNAL CABIN
AT
CHURCH MANOR WAY CROSSING (No. 4)
(Between Plumstead and Abbey Wood Stations).

MONDAY, JANUARY 1st, 1917.

On Monday, January 1st, 1917, a New Halt (situated 71 chains on the Dartford side of Plumstead Station), and served by Loop Lines from the existing Down and Up North Kent Lines, will be opened for Passenger Traffic, and will be known as Church Manor Way Halt.

A New Signal Cabin, to be known as Plumstead "C" Cabin, situated on the Down side of the Line 230 yards on the Dartford side of Church Manor Way Level Crossing, will also be brought into use at the same time.

Plumstead Station Cabin will in future be known as Plumstead "A" Cabin, and Plumstead Goods Sidings Cabin as Plumstead "B" Cabin.

For Complete List of New and Altered Signals, also Diagram of Lines, see following pages.

Front page of the SECR Permanent Way Working Notice, which announced the opening of Church Manorway Halt.

Eltham Well Hall

Opened as Well Hall (Bexley Heath Railway): 1.5.1895.
Received the suffix "& North Eltham" (South Eastern & Chatham Railway): 1.10.1916.
The suffix was also shown as "For North Eltham".
Received final name (Southern Railway): 26.9.1927.
Sometimes shown as Eltham (Well Hall)
Resited (British Rail): 17.3.1985.

Well Hall station looking east in the early years of the twentieth century. Well Hall itself was an old mansion, which dated from 1730 and stood to the north of the station until its demolition in 1930.

One of the original stations on the 8mile 44.46chains Bexley Heath Railway, which linked Blackheath with Dartford, Well Hall opened with the line on 1st May 1895. It comprised two platforms and, when inspected by Major Marindin on behalf of the Board of Trade, was stated as having a signal box with fifteen levers, of which two were spare. The inspection report, which was written on 5th April 1895, gave no other specific details of Well Hall, but said that minor work at all the stations needed to be completed, including the fitting of external clocks, the finishing of approaches and the lettering on doors.

Originally it seems that a crossover was provided between both passenger lines adjoining the platforms, but this was taken out of use in January 1902 and replaced by a crossover at either end. At this time, the signal box was described as having nineteen working levers and one spare.

The advent of a new station at Eltham Park, less than half-a-mile to the east threatened the possibility of closure, but this was ruled out by a clause in an earlier agreement with land-owner Sir Henry Page-Turner Barron, so it remained open. He insisted that the line had to skirt the southern boundary of his estate and even stipulated the exact site of the station. This deviation necessitated a sharp 12 chain curve immediately west of Well Hall, which was subjected to a speed restriction of 20mph.

As the years progressed and more houses were constructed in the vicinity, it became clear that both stations could serve a useful purpose. To accommodate the influx of building materials, the number of sidings at Well Hall was increased from three to six in 1915, when an average total of seventy-five wagon-loads were being handled every day. The sidings also proved useful for the accommodation of ambulance trains conveying wounded servicemen en-route to a nearby hospital.

In 1916 the station was re-named Well Hall & North Eltham, then soon after the line was electrified, it became Eltham Well Hall during 1927. As a prelude to electrification, the platforms were extended to 520ft in 1924-5 and a footbridge was erected. A limited number of electric trains began operating the line on 10th May 1926, but another two months passed before the full service was introduced on 19th July.

In 1930, the Southern Railway decided to carry out further station improvements along the line, with the Board allocating over £21,000 for alterations at Eltham Well Hall, Welling, Bexleyheath and Barnehurst. The work at Eltham Well Hall included a new main building on the up side, which was constructed of red brick beneath a red tiled roof. This was accessed by the existing approach from Well Hall Road, but a supplementary entrance was also provided on the down side. The canopy on the up platform was damaged during the Second World War and was still awaiting repair a decade later. The timber waiting shelter opposite, which had escaped the 1930s rebuilding and is thought to have dated from 1895 seems to have remained unscathed, however.

The eastern ends of the platforms were extended around 1953 to accommodate ten-car trains and an electrical sub-station was commissioned in the goods yard during 1955. This replaced an earlier utility at Eltham Park, which was then closed and demolished two years later. The yard itself, which had functioned since the line opened, fell into disuse from 7th October 1968 and was lifted, although a short refuge siding was subsequently laid on the site. The signal box, which stood at the London end of the down platform, virtually opposite the yard, remained in use a little longer, but eventually succumbed on 15th March 1970, as part of a re-signalling scheme.

On 11th June 1972, a returning excursion train conveying railway staff from Margate to London took the 12 chain curve at excessive speed and derailed, thereby causing the deaths of six people including the driver.

The construction of the Rochester Way Relief Road in the 1980s resulted in the station being closed and replaced by a new one, named simply Eltham, immediately to the east. The new station, with platforms contiguous with its predecessor, was funded as part of the road project and brought into use on 17th March 1985. From this date Eltham Well Hall was abandoned and in a short while was completely demolished.

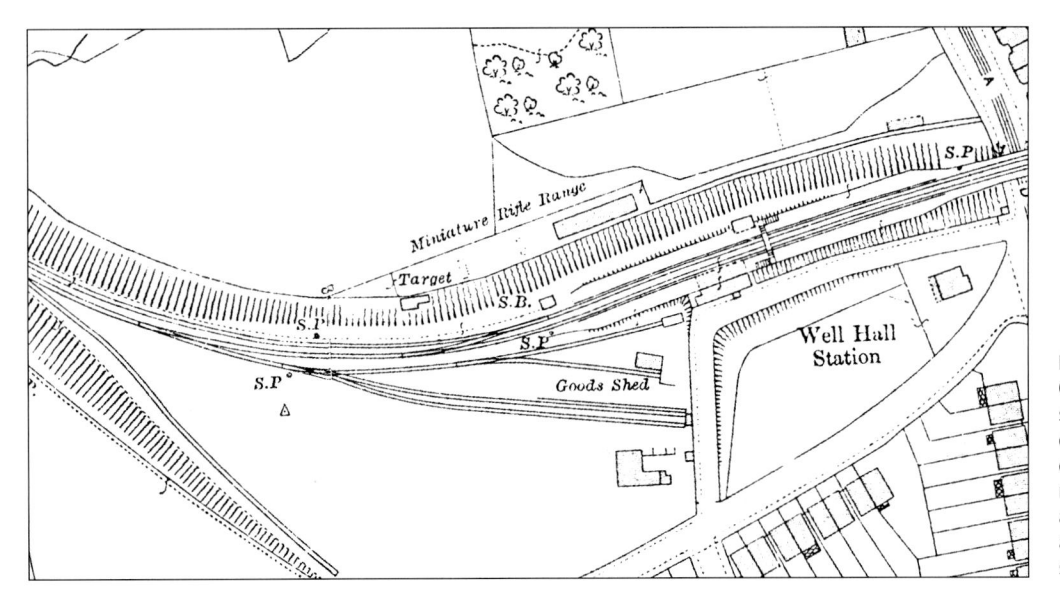

Extract from the 1:2500 Ordnance Survey map of 1916, showing the passenger station on the right and the goods yard on the left. Around 1907, a five roomed house was erected at the foot of the up side approach to accommodate the station master and his family.

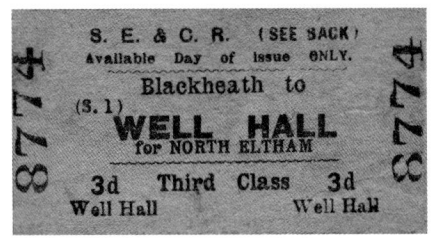

A selection of tickets: *Left:* SECR Third Class single from Blackheath to Well Hall for North Eltham issued 18th July 1925. *Centre:* British Railways Third Class single from Eltham Well Hall to Cannon Street or London Bridge issued 21st May 1954. *Right:* British Railways Board Eltham Well Hall platform ticket issued 18th May 1968.

Above: Well Hall station, looking east from the up platform at an unknown date, after electrification, showing the footbridge which was erected in the mid-1920s.

Right: In this view, dating from January 1975, we see the main building, as reconstructed by the Southern Railway in the 1930s. It led onto the up platform and was accessed by means of a short approach located on the west side of Well Hall Road.

Eltham Well Hall – 67

Top left: The exterior of the 1930s main building at Eltham Well Hall, viewed from its eastern end on 3rd January 1975.

Lower left: The interior of the booking hall, seen on the same day.

Below: The main building, looking east on 1st March 1976, showing the replacement canopy which was erected following Second World War bomb damage. There were a number of air raid incidents in the area during this period, although not all these affected the station itself. Of those that did, the most serious happened on 3rd August and 14th November 1944. The log for the first incident recorded that at 1.15am, the station buildings and signal box were badly damaged. The record for 14th November stated that a V2 rocket landed 200 yards from the line, causing further damage and injuring fifteen people. It seems likely that the damage sustained to the canopy of the main building occurred during the raid of 3rd August.

Top right: Considering the fact that much of the station had been modernised, the survival of a South Eastern Railway waiting shelter on the down side at Eltham Well Hall was perhaps surprising. During the rebuilding its central opening was provided with a glazed screen, as seen in this view, which was taken just before closure.

Lower right: This view looks east from the down platform in March 1985 and includes the main building on the right and the earlier waiting shelter to the left. Beyond the footbridge can be seen the small down side exit and, in the distance, the present Eltham station which was then being prepared for opening.

Below: After closure little time was wasted in the demolition of Eltham Well Hall. This view, taken on 18th May 1985, shows the main building after the removal of its roof, windows and various fittings.

Eltham Park

Opened as Shooter's Hill & Eltham Park (South Eastern & Chatham Railway): 1.7.1908.
Received final name (Southern Railway): 26.9.1927.
Closed (British Rail): 17.3.1985.

The street level building at Shooter's Hill & Eltham Park station, as it appeared soon after opening in 1908. According to an engineer's drawing, the front and side walls were to be constructed of first class Gault bricks, but second class bricks were deemed suitable for the rear.

In 1899, the developer, Cameron Corbett purchased a 334 acre site east of Well Hall station and within a short while work started on an estate of suburban villas. He approached the SECR with a view to providing a station to serve the new houses and, having offered to provide the company with financial assistance, agreement was reached on 13th October 1900.

As part of the scheme, the SECR was to close Well Hall and provide replacement premises on the east side of what is now Westmount Road. This however, contravened part of the original Bexley Heath Railway agreement, so the Company reluctantly informed Corbett that the idea had to be scrapped. The developer nevertheless remained adamant that the new station was essential for his estate and sued the railway for breach of contract. Damages were awarded in May 1905 and the Company had to accept the idea of having two stations serving the district, which were spaced at less than half a mile apart.

The new premises, described in the 1900 agreement as offering *"superior passenger accommodation"* were designed by the SECR architect Alfred William Blomfield and were to be built on a gradient of 1 in 80 falling towards Well Hall. On 26th March 1907, the SECR wrote to the Board of Trade, asking whether there would be any objection to this and added that the expense of flattening the gradient might prohibit the work taking place. Unfortunately, the reply does not appear to have survived, but clearly all was well, as a contract for the station's construction was subsequently awarded to G.E. Wallis & Sons Ltd of Broadmead Works, Maidstone. The estimated cost was £12,488 and the SECR insisted that the work had to be completed by 31st May 1908, with no extension of time being allowed. Rather confusingly, the wording of the contract showed the name of the premises as *"Well Hall"*, although by this date it is unlikely that the Company were still hoping to close the original, as previously intended. It stated that the work entailed the *"Construction of a new station at Well Hall between the bridges carrying the roads over the railway known as Westmount Road and Glenesk Road together with the widening of the bridge under the Westmount Road and the station buildings with bridge and gangways leading down to the platforms at that bridge."*

Work progressed well and on 17th June 1908, the Company wrote again to the Board of Trade stating that the station, which was to be named Shooter's Hill & Eltham Park, was ready for inspection.

Major Pringle was duly appointed and he visited the new premises on 22nd June. His report dated 2nd July gave the following description; *"There are two platforms, for the service of Up and Down trains respectively, and separate covered approaches have been arranged to each platform from the public road overbridge. Each platform is 450ft long by 16ft (wide) by 3ft in height. There are Ladies and General waiting rooms, together with conveniences for both sexes on each platform, and adequate accommodation has I think been provided.*

The platforms are lighted sufficiently and name boards fixed. The booking hall and office, which are not yet quite completed, are on the high level, carried on an extension/widening of the public road overbridge.

There are no sidings or connections of any sort and no additional signalling beyond that at the two adjoining stations. Some of the existing signals require to have their positions altered, then the down advance Starting signal from Well Hall Station would I think be better placed on the Well Hall side of the public footway crossing."

Major Pringle stated that all unfinished work needed completion, but otherwise had no objection to the station opening, which was just as well, as trains started to call on the day before his report was written! His various requirements were nevertheless implemented and on 6th November 1908, the SECR informed the Board of Trade that everything had been done.

In 1922 a footbridge was erected towards the London end and a booking office provided on the up platform. Once this was operational, the street level building was closed and converted into shops, subsequently named 'Station Parade'.

The line was electrified in 1926 and a substation was erected a little to the east of the down platform. The following year the station was renamed Eltham Park, but otherwise remained little altered for the rest of its days.

Soon after nationalisation in 1948, the newly formed British Railways began to explore the possibilities of finding a new source of power, as the existing equipment, dating from 1926, was becoming time-expired. In November 1950, a scheme was approved whereby current for the line would be taken from the British Electric Authority's Deptford Power Station and fed to a transformer at Lewisham. From here it passed to sub-stations at Eltham Well Hall and Bexleyheath, which were built specifically for the purpose. They were brought into use during 1955 and the earlier pair which served the route were made redundant. One was retained and put to other uses, but the building at Eltham Park was demolished in 1957. Four years earlier, the platforms were lengthened to take ten-car trains, with the up side extension being constructed at the country end. The old sub-station remained in use at the time however and stood close to the existing platform, so the down side had to be extended at the London end instead.

During the early 1980s, the construction of the Rochester Way Relief Road resulted in the need for Well Hall to be resited. As the new premises were located east of the original, closure of Eltham Park became an inevitable option. The last train departed at 00.08 on 17th March 1985 and, despite attempts by a group of enthusiasts to save the buildings and their distinctive SECR awnings, demolition came soon after. The former booking hall in Westmount Road continues to serve as shops and has acquired local listed status. In April 2003, its cast iron downpipe hoppers continued to show the date of construction and the name "Station Parade' was still displayed on the building's frontage. Down below, the derelict and part-demolished platforms remained evident and are perhaps best viewed, albeit at a distance, from the bridge carrying Glenesk Road above the tracks.

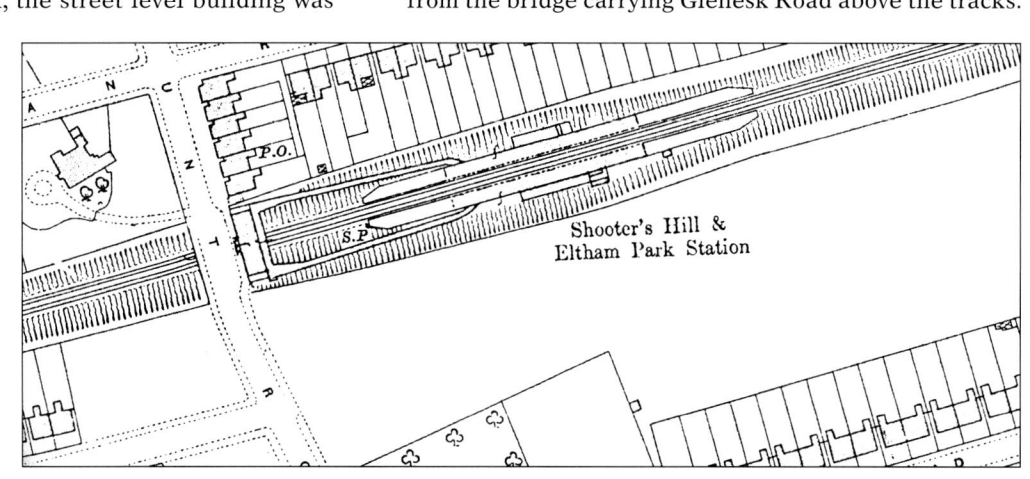

Extract of the 1:2500 Ordnance Survey map of 1916 showing Shooter's Hill & Eltham Park station at the centre.

Left: The street level building whilst still fairly new, with public telephone signs hanging from beneath the entrance canopy and a Corbett Estates board beyond the parade of shops on the left.

Below: A view of the station soon after opening, looking from the ramp which led from the street level building to the up platform.

Right: Looking southwards along the down platform at Shooter's Hill & Eltham Park around 1912, with the bridge carrying Glenesk Road visible in the distance.

Below: The rear of the street level building as it appeared in 1973, showing the western extension of the down platform carried out twenty years earlier. BR totem type name tablets can be seen on the two lamp posts on the right. These presumably dated from when the platform was extended, although as new boards had to be provided, it seems a little strange that the station was not completely re-signed at the time, as Southern Railway targets were retained elsewhere on the station.

Eltham Park – 73

Above: Looking west along the up platform in 1973, with a SR 'target' name tablet on the lamp post to the right.

Below: An eastward view taken on the same day, with the footbridge added in 1922 spanning above the line.

Above: Looking west along the up side in October 1984, with the 1953 platform extension in the foreground. To the left can be seen an empty space on top of the concrete fencing where a running-in nameboard had previously been situated.

Right: A general view of the station, looking west from the down platform in October 1984.

Below: Southern Railway 3rd Class single ticket issued from Blackheath on 26th October 1925.

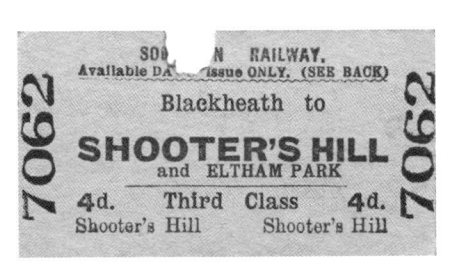

Eltham Park – 75

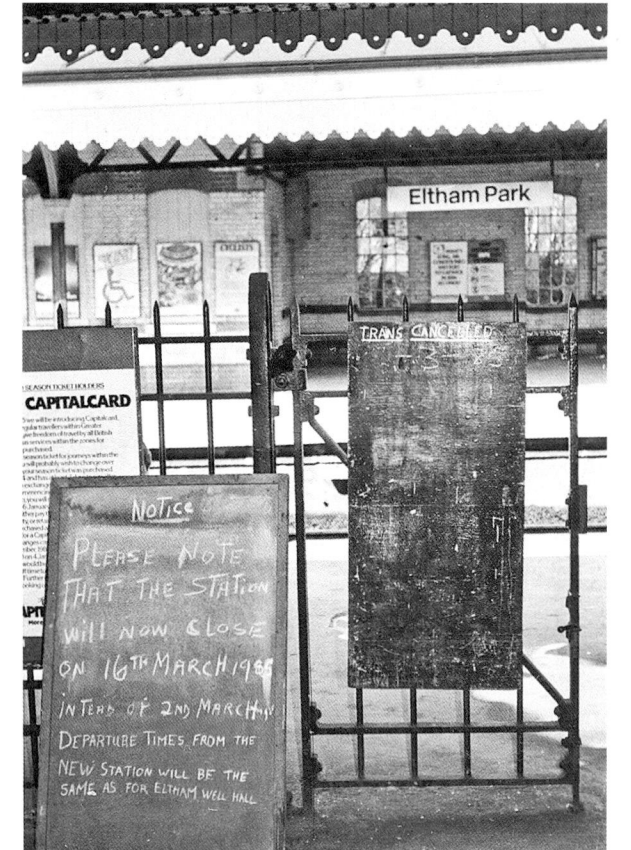

Left: Closure was to take place after the end of traffic on 2nd March 1985, but this was delayed because construction of the replacement Eltham station was still under way. A revised date was therefore announced and was shown on this notice board alongside the ticket office.

Right: SECR Third Class single ticket issued to Lewisham Junction on 7th August 1923.

Right: British Railways platform ticket issued on 15th January 1956.

Below: Eltham Park station, looking west in falling snow shortly before closure.

76 – London's Disused Railway Stations – Outer South East London

Above: Looking east from the station footbridge in October 1984.

Right: The street level building in March 1985, with roadworks in progress to the right.

Eltham Park – 77

Above and left: Two views of the disused Eltham Park station taken in December 1985, after the platforms had been partially demolished. By this time the platform buildings and awnings had gone completely, leaving just parts of the ramps which once provided access to and from street level.

Below: British Railways Board platform ticket issued on 9th February 1985.

Chislehurst

Opened as Chislehurst & Bickley Park (South Eastern Railway): 1.7.1865.
Suffix dropped (South Eastern Railway): 1.9.1866.
Resited (South Eastern Railway): 2.3.1868 (probably).

The temporary terminus of the SER main line towards Sevenoaks, Chislehurst & Bickley Park station was constructed during the early part of 1865. On 7th April of that year the Company wrote to the Board of Trade stating that it wished to give one month's notice of opening the first portion of the *"Lewisham and Tunbridge* (sic) *Line between the Greenwich Junction and Chislehurst"*. An additional communication written twenty days later included the relevant plans and stated that the Engineer felt that all would be completed by Monday 8th May.

Colonel Yolland was duly appointed to inspect the works and his report, which was dated 11th May 1865 stated that the length of line from *"the Greenwich Junction to Chislehurst was 6 miles 64 chains."*

Of the terminus he wrote: *" ... the temporary station at Chislehurst has only a single platform, from which all trains are to depart and to arrive, involving the use of facing points; but I understand that the trains will not be numerous and that the engine bringing a Train in, will take the next Train out. As a temporary measure this may be sanctioned. The permanent Station for Chislehurst is intended to be some short distance further down the line ...* " He went on to state: *"An engine turntable is to be put up at Chislehurst Station ... "*, but although the brickwork of the well had been completed, little else had been done. Because of this and a few other problems elsewhere along the route he refused to sanction opening. However he paid a second visit on 2nd June and his report, written that day, stated that although some small items still needed attention, he had no further objections to the line being brought into public use.

Opening took place on 1st July and the station served as a terminus for nearly three years. Meanwhile work on the extension continued and on 3rd February 1868, freight traffic was extended along the new metals to Sevenoaks. The replacement Chislehurst station, sited south-east of the original, was brought into use a month later and its predecessor was closed. The nearby goods yard, which had opened with the temporary terminus, remained in use however and survived until 18th November 1968.

Apart from details included in the inspection report, little appears to have been recorded about the station, so further information is rather sketchy. It is known that it was located *"in the vicinity of the goods yard"*, but precise details seem to be uncertain.

The present road named Old Hill was previously known as 'Old Station Hill'. Near the west end of this, on the northern side of Chislehurst Road, a brick building adjoining the line has been claimed in the past as once serving the station. There can be little doubt that its appearance suggests this possibility, but it seems rather substantial for something which was intended to be temporary, and no map or plan has been located which can confirm its origin.

Lower Sydenham

Opened (Mid Kent Railway): 1.1.1857.
Resited (South Eastern & Chatham Railway): 1906.

Lower Sydenham was one of the original stations on the Mid Kent Railway and opened with the route to Beckenham on 1st January 1857. When surveyed in 1894 it comprised two platforms, which were linked at the country end by means of a footbridge. A small shelter stood on the up side, but the main building faced the down platform and was accessed by means of an approach which led south from Southend Lane. To the north of this building lay a goods yard, which comprised a single siding and headshunt, controlled by a signal box which adjoined the up line.

The passenger station was subsequently resited about 100yds to the south, although the goods yard remained as before. The new premises were inspected on behalf of the Board of Trade by Col. J.W. Pringle on 15th October 1906 and his report written two days later stated that the replacement platforms each had a length of 200yds and a booking office had been provided on both sides. He stated that a new signal box, containing eighteen working levers and two spare had been erected, but unfortunately gave no details of the earlier premises.

Once the new station was operational, the original premises were removed, although the goods and coal yard, which was convenient for a nearby gasworks, continued to function until 20th June 1966. By this time however, supplies for the gas works were being conveyed by road.

New Beckenham

Opened (Mid Kent Railway): 1.4.1864.
Resited (South Eastern Railway): c1868.

Partly subsidised by the nearby Cator Estate, the first New Beckenham station opened with the Mid Kent Railway Addiscombe Road extension on 1st April 1864. It was located south of the junction with the original MKR route to Beckenham and was provided with a substantial yellow brick building facing the up Addiscombe Road line. This rose to a height of two storeys and included both the ticket office and living accommodation for the Stationmaster. The first edition Ordnance Survey map shows the premises to have been completely surrounded by open countryside and accessed only by means of a footpath, as Bridge Road which now crosses the southern end of the site was not authorised until August 1897.

Initially, Addiscombe Road and Beckenham Junction trains operated separately to and from central London, but after a short while it was decided to combine these, with the portions either splitting or joining at New Beckenham, depending on direction of travel. Unfortunately the existing layout at New Beckenham made such changes unworkable, so a new station was planned 9 chains north of the junction.

This was duly constructed and the original premises closed, although the actual date of completion seems uncertain. In his *Chronology of London's Railways*, H.V. Borley shows "*c.1868*", but original documentation hints that the change may have taken place two years earlier. The platforms were subsequently largely removed, but the main building survived as a private house and continued as such into the twenty-first century.

It was vacated around 2001 when adjoining land was being prepared for residential development, but although partially boarded-up to deter vandals, it remained standing until June 2003. Having stood for the best part of 137 years since closure, the original New Beckenham was undoubtedly one of Greater London's longest lived disused stations.

Right: Extract from the First Edition OS map, surveyed in 1861, but amended ten years later and published in 1883. As can be seen, the original New Beckenham station is shown as closed. The long-lived house is included, along with two platforms, but no other buildings are evident. Originally it was intended to construct platforms on both routes, but this plan was subsequently altered and New Beckenham was built to serve the Addiscombe Road line only. It is understood that a small shelter was located on the down side, but this does not appear on the map so it was presumably demolished soon after closure. The line curving off to the south-east is the link to what is now Beckenham Junction.

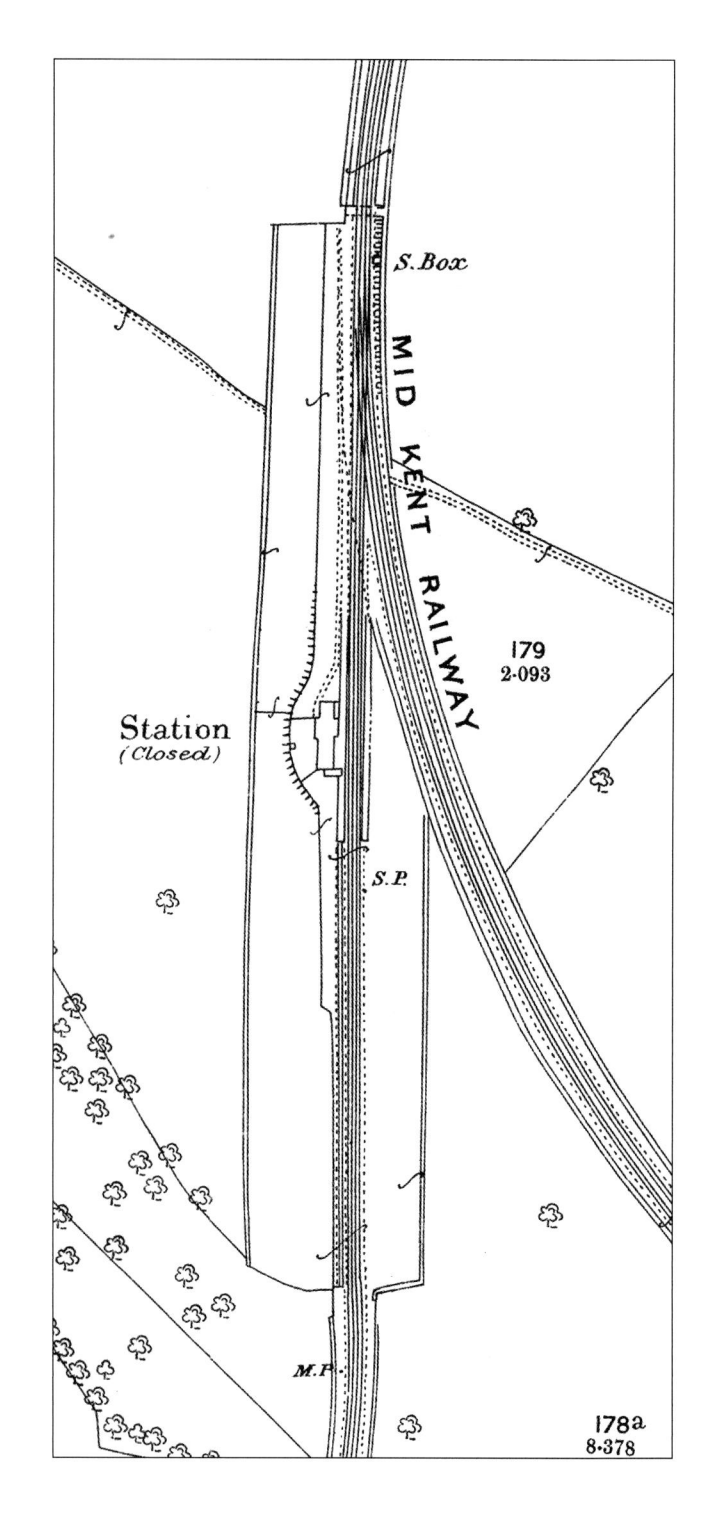

Right: The remains of the original New Beckenham station, viewed from the country end at an unknown date, possibly in the late 1930s. It was among three stations on the line built by the firm of Smith & Knight, who were awarded the contract on 27th March 1863.

Below: A 1973 view taken from Bridge Road, with the old station in the foreground and its replacement in the distance to the right. The offices and facilities were located in the single storey section closest to the camera, whilst the stationmaster lived in the adjoining house. At the time of its demolition in 2003, it was believed to be the oldest surviving disused station in Greater London.

Woodside

Opened (South Eastern Railway): 1871.
Named Woodside & South Norwood
(South Eastern & Chatham Railway / Southern Railway): 1.10.1908 - 2.10.1944.
Closed (Railtrack): 2.6.1997.
South end of site now incorporates the Croydon Tramlink Woodside tram stop.
Sometimes referred to as Woodside (Surrey)

The street level building at Woodside in pre-grouping days. The doorway in the centre was the entrance, whilst either side of the frontage were exits.

Woodside station was located 69ch from Addiscombe Road on the line from Elmers End and opened in 1871. It was built to serve the growing suburban district of South Norwood and the Croydon Racecourse which was located nearby.

It seems that the station was initially a simple affair and remained unaltered until 1884 when a bay was added on the down side to accommodate trains using the Woodside & South Croydon Joint Railway which had just been constructed.

Major General Hutchinson inspected the new line on behalf of the Board of Trade and his report, written on 24th October 1884, made it quite clear that he was dissatisfied with the work carried out at Woodside itself. He insisted that a footbridge or subway was constructed to allow passengers safe access between platforms and also objected to the fact that the only shelter available was on the up side.

The South Eastern Railway wrote to the Board of Trade on 7th November 1884, asking if it would grant opening of the line if the required improvements were carried out at a later date, but the BoT remained adamant that the alterations should be carried out first. A month later, the Company secretary wrote again, stating that alternative plans had been drawn up for the station. It was now to be completely rebuilt with a booking office above the tracks facing *"the highway from Norwood to Bromley"*. From here, stairs would descend to the platforms and also serve as a footbridge. More adequate shelter would be provided and the entire work was expected to take about three months. It was clearly a more expensive exercise than had been anticipated, but the Directors finally gave it their approval and the Civil Engineer was instructed to start work immediately.

Major General Hutchinson was now satisfied and, in his report dated 28th July 1885, he wrote: *"Woodside station has been reconstructed and provided with excellent accommodation including means for passing between the up and down platforms without crossing the rails on the level."*

The premises were constructed largely in yellow brick and were clearly an improvement on those which they replaced. There were three platform faces, which included the bay, whilst immediately to the south stood a signal box with twenty-three working levers and seven spare.

Woodside shared the same fortunes as Addiscombe Road and benefited from additional traffic created by Croydon Racecourse, which lay to the east of the line, until meetings ceased in 1890.

The Woodside & South Croydon Railway was never a financial success and closed at the beginning of 1917. The bay at Woodside fell into disuse and was never reinstated, although the line it was built to serve re-opened when electrified in 1935.

Apart from the loss of its bay, the station underwent little else in the way of physical change until the British Railways era when the platforms were extended to accommodate 10-car trains. The single-road coal yard, which lay behind the up platform and opened in the 1870s, eventually succumbed to road competition and closed on 30th September 1963. After closure of the yard, the main purpose of the signal box was to operate the junction with the Woodside & South Croydon line, but when this closed for the second time in 1983, it was of little further use and was abolished from 24th June 1984. The same decade also witnessed the shortening of the platform canopies, which had lost their decorative valancing some time before.

The street level building was eventually closed and passengers had to access the platforms by means of a former exit which led directly from the stairways. With no other booking facilities, a Permit to Travel machine was installed on the up side, but, with the station completely un-staffed, this soon fell foul of vandals.

Woodside closed after the last train on Saturday 31st May 1997 and its platforms were subsequently demolished during the construction of Croydon Tramlink. The new tram stop opened with the Beckenham route on Tuesday 23rd May 2000 and occupies the south end of the former station site. The stairway which previously led to the up platform has been adapted as means of access, but the 1885 street level building and down side stairs remained disused and by 2003 appeared derelict.

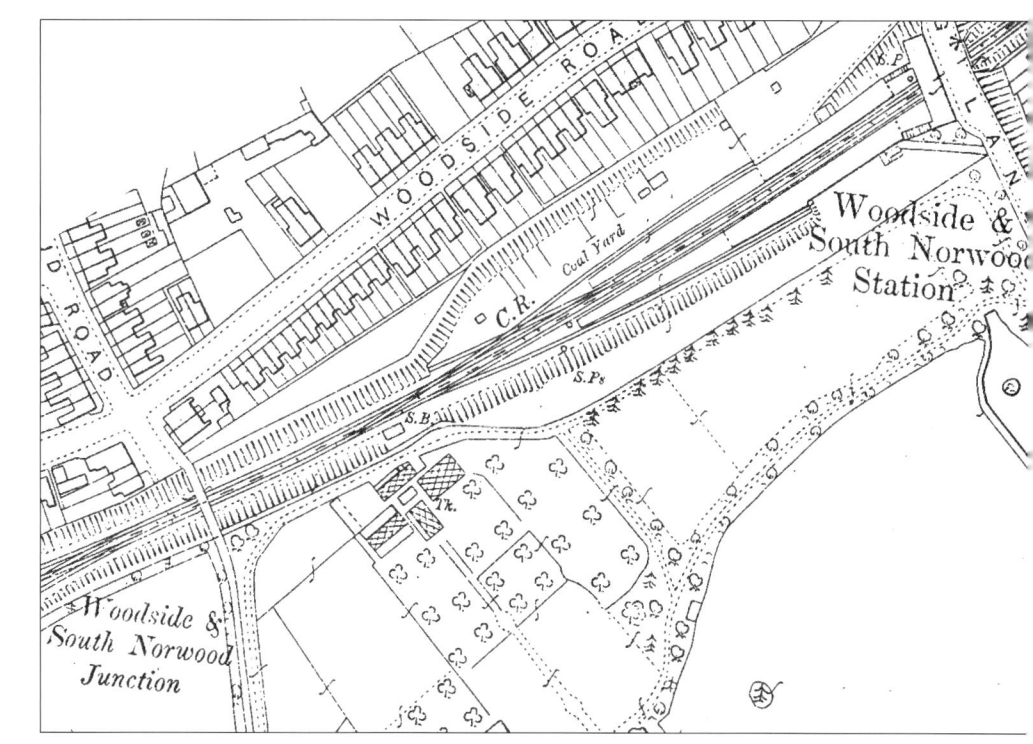

Extract from the Ordnance Survey 1:2500 map of 1912, showing Woodside station on the right and the junction to the left. The small coal yard appears behind the up platform and was accessed from the western side of Spring Lane, a little to the north of the station building. On the opposite side of the line, a sloping footpath connected the down platform to the southernmost exit.

Above: An SECR Kitson steam railmotor, designed by Harry Wainwright stands at the Woodside bay platform in the early twentieth century whilst working the service to Selsdon Road.

Left: The 6.31pm train from Cannon Street is seen arriving at Woodside on 19th July 1951, led by ex-Southern Railway 4-SUB unit No 4508. At the time, the 'T' headcode signified that the service was bound for Addiscombe.

Right: The street level building at Woodside, seen from its south-eastern end at an unknown date, possibly in the early 1960s. The exit closest to the camera had been bricked-up, but that serving the up side appears to have still been in use.

Below: The building as it appeared in the mid-1970s, after the former up side exit had also been bricked-up.

Woodside – 85

Above: An interior view of the booking hall at Woodside, looking towards the entrance doorway and front windows on 18th October 1982.

Left: The ticket office seen on the same day, with the doorway leading towards the down platform visible on the left.

Right: The doorway seen in the lower view reproduced opposite led onto a short section which was roofed over with corrugated iron. However, when this photograph was taken, much of the roofing had been removed, leaving just the section protecting the down side stairs as seen here. The door facing the camera led through to the former exit.

Below: The down side stairway at Woodside, viewed from platform level in October 1983.

Above: The north-eastern end of the down platform in October 1983, showing the roofing fitted to both stairway and the short section of walkway leading to the ticket hall.

Left: The down platform at Woodside, viewed from its Addiscombe end in October 1983.

88 – London's Disused Railway Stations – Outer South East London

Right: A general view of Woodside station, looking towards Elmers End in October 1983.

Below: The base of the up side stairway photographed at the same time, with the ticket collectors' box in the foreground.

Woodside – 89

Above and left: The exterior and interior of Woodside signal box, photographed in February 1980.

Right: Southern Railway Third Class single ticket to Elmers End issued on 24th February 1942.

Right: Undated British Railways Woodside platform ticket.

90 – London's Disused Railway Stations – Outer South East London

Above: Woodside station on the last day of railway traffic, 31st May 1997. The up line had been out of action since a fire destroyed the signal box at Addiscombe in March 1996 and by this time it had become overgrown.

Right: The rear of the street level building in May 1997, showing the now roofless up side stairway on the left.

Woodside – 91

Addiscombe

Opened as Addiscombe Road (Mid Kent Railway): 1.4.1864.
Received final name (Southern Railway): 1.4.1925.
Closed: (Railtrack): 2.6.1997.
Sometimes referred to as: Croydon (Addiscombe Road): 1.4.1864 - 1.4.1925,
Croydon (Addiscombe): 1.4.1925 - 3.1926 and Addiscombe (Croydon): 3.1926 - 13.6.1955.

The terminus at Addiscombe as it appeared in the mid-1970s. Although the station opened in 1864, the building seen here dated from the late nineteenth century.

The Elmers End - Addiscombe branch owed its origins to the South Eastern Railway wishing to have a direct route into Croydon. In 1861, the Company jointly promoted a Bill with the Mid Kent Railway to construct a 3mile 29chain double track branch from Beckenham to a terminus in Addiscombe Road. This received the Royal Assent on 17th July 1862 and Messrs. Smith & Knight were appointed as contractors.

Work was completed in a little under two years, although progress was hampered by the weather. *The Railway Times* of 13th February 1864 stated *"The works on the Addiscombe extension have been unexpectedly delayed by the wet autumn, but the line is now practically completed and will be opened in the course of the month."* This proved to be correct because by March 1864 the company informed the Board of Trade that the line was ready for inspection. Captain Rich, the inspecting officer, recorded that the formation had an overall width of 30ft throughout and that it was laid with 71lb double-headed rail in lengths of 21 and 24 feet. There were five overbridges, of which one was constructed entirely of brick, whilst the others were built around cast iron girders. The same material was used on the under bridges, except for that which carried the London Chatham & Dover line above the branch south of Beckenham, which employed the use of wrought iron. At the time of inspection, all work had been completed, with the exception of certain buffer-stops, although Captain Rich was assured that these would be erected without delay. Captain Rich felt that the track work left a little to be desired and that the stations would benefit from higher platforms, but otherwise had no objection to the route being opened for traffic. This was duly implemented and trains began operating into Addiscombe Road from 1st April.

When first promoted in 1855, the Mid-Kent Railway made an agreement with the South Eastern Railway that the larger company would work the line in return for a percentage of its gross receipts. This arrangement continued until July 1864, when a Bill was passed allowing the SER to purchase the MKR outright.

At the time of the line's opening, the area between Beckenham and Croydon was largely undeveloped, so the only intermediate station originally provided was at Elmers End. Beyond here, the tracks crossed the border from Kent into Surrey, then continued through open countryside. For the first 1 mile 748yards it climbed at 1 in 120, but then eased to 1 in 300 for the final stretch into the terminus.

THE STATION AS BUILT
Addiscombe Road station was provided with two platforms, of which that on the up side was an island. At the southern end stood the main building which was set back a short distance from the road and was accessed by means of an approach. The track serving the west side of the island terminated short at buffer stops adjoining the end wall of the building, but the main pair stretched a little further and ended at a turntable used for releasing incoming locomotives. From its layout it seems likely that all trains departed from the island, whilst the platform on the down side was used for arrivals only. Judging from the OS plan of 1868, this was completely devoid of shelter and continued to an exit which led directly onto the street. According to the plan this did not have an accompanying building of any substance, but presumably it may have been provided with a hut for the ticket collector.

The station was less than a mile from Croydon town centre and its immediate surroundings were in the process of being developed. Much of the local land had become available following the demolition of the Royal Military College for the East Indian Army, which had closed in 1862. The map of 1868 showed the immediate environs still largely open, with a brickfield to the west of the formation. Some villas had been erected on Morland Road, whilst

Addiscombe Road station in the late 19th century. Although of poor technical quality, the photograph has been included because of its rarity.

to the east of the line stood *The Alma* public house and a sprinkling of habitations in Grant Road.

Having reached Croydon, the South Eastern Railway then set its eyes on the districts which lay beyond and proposed an extension towards Red Hill. This was successfully opposed by the London, Brighton & South Coast Railway however and the scheme was eventually dropped.

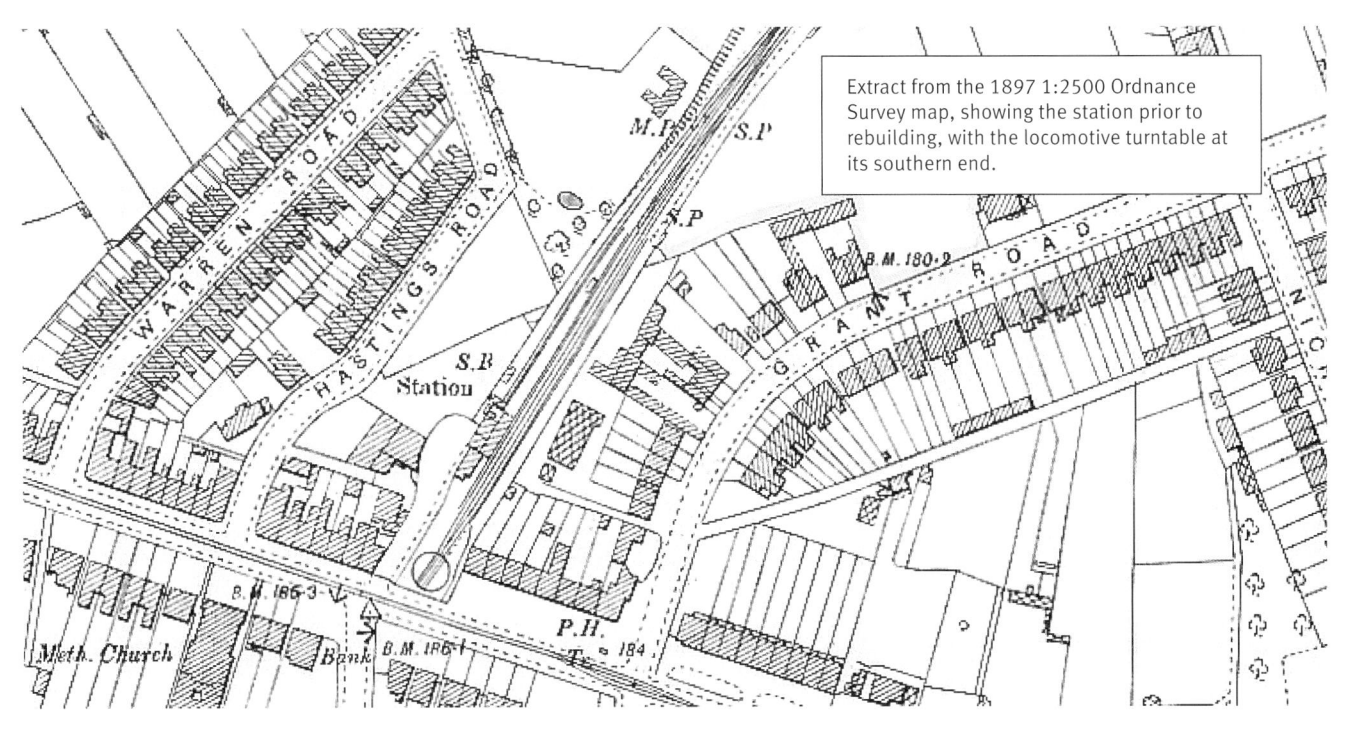

Extract from the 1897 1:2500 Ordnance Survey map, showing the station prior to rebuilding, with the locomotive turntable at its southern end.

NINETEENTH CENTURY SERVICES

The initial Addiscombe Road service ran on weekdays only and comprised eleven trains in both directions. By the following March, the number had increased to sixteen, but the line was not used on Sundays.

The operating pattern was completely revised in 1866, when trains from London would split at New Beckenham, with one portion continuing to Addiscombe Road and the other to Beckenham Junction. The reverse procedure took place in the opposite direction, but the existing layout made this difficult to work. Therefore the SER decided to close the existing New Beckenham station and replace it with a new one 9chains north of the junction between the two lines. (See page 84)

Operational conditions were further improved in the early twentieth century, when a central runround loop was added at New Beckenham and therefore incoming locomotives could be released with greater ease. The system of combining Addiscombe Road and Beckenham Junction trains remained in use until 1916, when it was dropped in favour of running separate services to both destinations.

SERVICE EXPANSION
AND A SHORT-LIVED EAST END CONNECTION

From 1st April 1880, the SER began operating a service of sixteen trains between Addiscombe Road and the Great Eastern Railway terminus at Liverpool Street. These ran by way of new connecting spurs onto the East London Line near New Cross and thence through the Thames Tunnel.

With the opening of the St. Mary's Curve on 3rd March 1884, the service was re-routed into St. Mary's (Whitechapel), where movements were controlled by a twelve lever signal box at the junction and a four lever cabin at the station itself. This arrangement proved to be short lived however, as the last SER train between Addiscombe Road and St. Mary's (Whitechapel) ran on 30th September 1884, when the ownership of the Curve was transferred from the East London Railway to the Joint Committee of the Metropolitan and Metropolitan District companies. Details of St. Mary's (Whitechapel) may be found in *London's Disused Underground Stations* by the same author.

By the following year, there were twenty-five weekday trains each way between Addiscombe Road and central London, with four on Sundays. The service over the northern part of the line was further increased by the opening of the Woodside & South Croydon Joint Railway on 10th August 1885. *(See Bingham Road, Coombe Road, Selsdon and Spencer Road Halt)*.

STATION REBUILDING

By 1897, the area around Addiscombe Road station had become much more built-up, with residential developments on both sides of the line. To the west lay Warren Road and Hastings Road, both occupying the site of the former brickfield, whilst to the east, the longer established Grant Road had become virtually lined with housing.

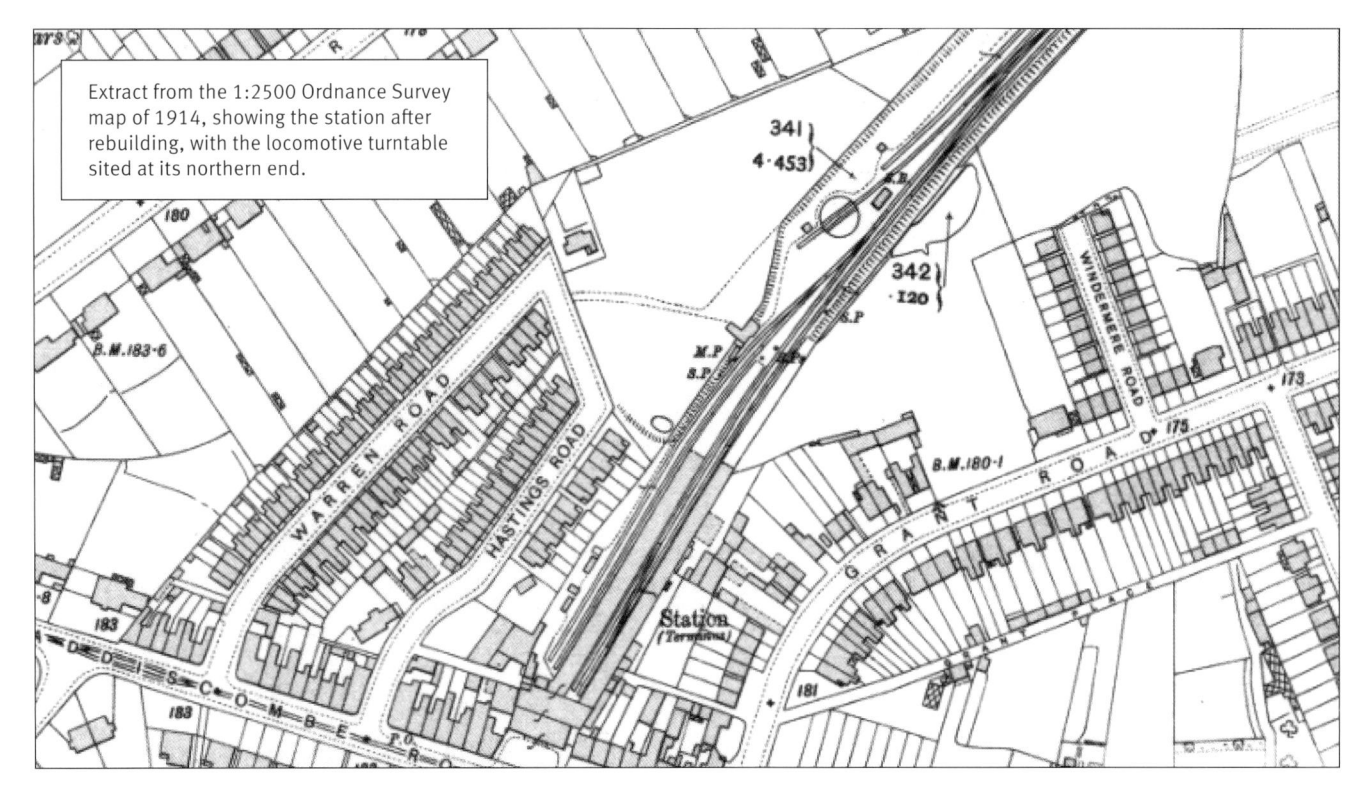

Extract from the 1:2500 Ordnance Survey map of 1914, showing the station after rebuilding, with the locomotive turntable sited at its northern end.

The exterior of Addiscombe Road station after its 1899 rebuilding, with wrought ironwork in evidence on top of the central roof and upon the wall separating the forecourt from the street.

A little later it was decided that the terminus should be rebuilt and work was soon under way.

The station was larger than before and comprised a red-brick main building which faced onto Lower Addiscombe Road. This was provided with a gated forecourt and the new arrangement occupied the site previously used by the turntable. As turning facilities were still deemed necessary, a replacement table was constructed at the opposite end of the premises, a little to the west of the running lines.

The main station building contained the booking hall and led onto a concourse, which in turn provided access to the trains. Again there was a side platform and an island, and these were both protected by substantial awnings. Because of the revised layout, the signalling arrangements had to be extensively altered and a new box was provided. This replaced the original and contained forty working levers with five spare. Once completed, the rebuilt premises were inspected by Colonel F.A. Marindin on behalf of the Board of Trade and approved for public use on 3rd August 1899.

EARLY TWENTIETH CENTURY PASSENGER SERVICES

For all these improvements however, Addiscombe Road could not hope to compete favourably with the nearby LBSCR station at East Croydon when it came to residential traffic. In 1910, the journey by stopping train into Cannon Street took around forty minutes, whilst services using the direct LBSCR reached central London much more quickly.

There were a few semi-fasts however, and just prior to the First World War, there was a service which was locally dubbed 'The Flyer'. This departed from Addiscombe Road at 7.20am then called only at Woodside before running non-stop to London Bridge and Cannon Street, where it terminated at 7.46am. By this time, the terminus was particularly busy, with thirty-nine weekday departures and thirty-seven arrivals.

ELECTRIFICATION

At the time of its absorption into the Southern Railway in 1923, the branch remained much as it had since the start of the century, but a radical change was now on its way.

With the spread of electrification throughout the SR suburban system during the early 1920s, consideration was given to extending East London Line trains beyond New Cross and terminating them at Addiscombe Road instead. The Metropolitan Railway was keen on the idea and during 1925 began to work out costings. A detailed study of the route and its existing services was carried

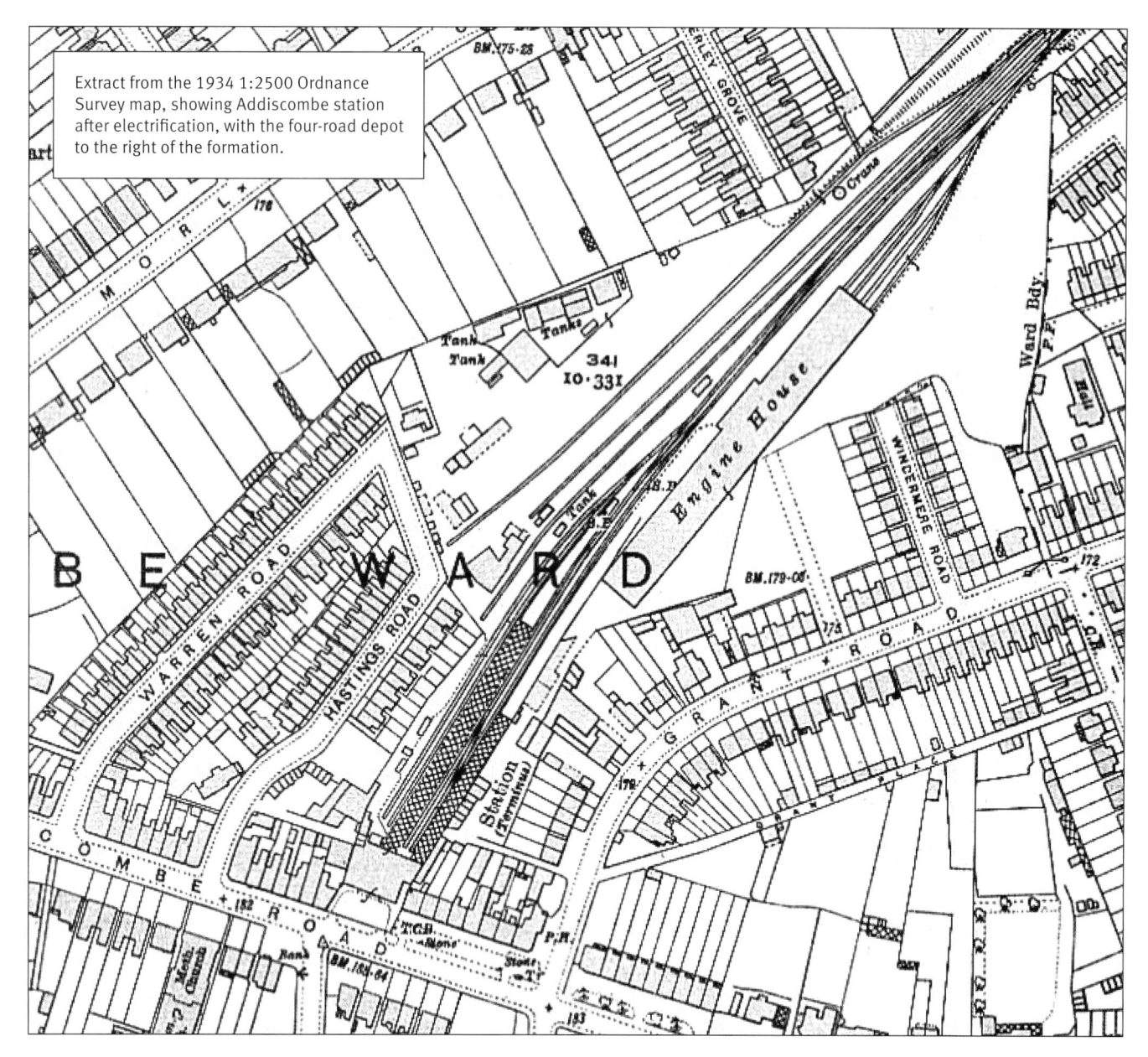

Extract from the 1934 1:2500 Ordnance Survey map, showing Addiscombe station after electrification, with the four-road depot to the right of the formation.

out, but the company was clearly not impressed. An internal memo of the time stated *"The present travelling facilities over the Addiscombe line are poor. The stations are old and dingy, the service is infrequent and unpunctual, and the stock used is old, dirty and in bad condition."* The Metropolitan proposed operating eight trains every hour for eight hours of the day linking Hammersmith with Addiscombe Road, but the scheme was beset by problems and despite much preparatory planning, it was abandoned in 1930.

In the meantime, the Southern Railway was pressing on with its own electrification programme and, whilst work was under way, the station was renamed Addiscombe on 1st April 1925. Electric trains were introduced to the branch on 28th February 1926, but the full service, which provided a half-hourly link with central London had to wait a further five months. The new mode of traction brought both speed and efficiency and semi-fasts completed the journey in twenty-five minutes.

To service the new units, a depot was erected on the east side of the line at Addiscombe and comprised four roads. The electric trains ran in four car sets, although these were soon reduced to three. To aid identification, both by passengers and staff, the Southern Railway introduced a series of letter codes which were displayed against an illuminated panel on the leading car. These took the form of metal stencils and varied from route to route. Services travelling to Addiscombe were denoted by the letter 'T', which either appeared in its plain form, or with a bar above if the train was routed via Parks Bridge Junction.

THE SECOND WORLD WAR AND AFTER
At the beginning of 1939, the Addiscombe service remained half hourly. However the coming of war in September of that year was to bring drastic reductions and the branch never really recovered.

Emergency cuts in passenger services brought in from 16th October 1939 resulted in Addiscombe being served by a shuttle to and from Elmers End only, with the route being closed completely for a period around mid-day except on Saturdays.

After the war, normality slowly returned, and by the spring of 1948, regular through trains were again running between Addiscombe and central London. On Sundays the service remained a shuttle, with connections being made with Hayes trains at Elmers End. By now however, traffic on the branch was declining, and from 1950 all through services were withdrawn. Trains working the shuttle were initially provided with the headcode '2', but this was later altered to '06' and in later years became just plain '6'.

A modernisation plan announced in 1955 authorised the extension of South Eastern Division suburban station platforms to 675ft so that they could accommodate ten-car trains and perhaps surprisingly, Addiscombe was included in the scheme. It was dealt with under '*Stage IV*' which also encompassed the routes linking Catford Bridge with Hayes, and Woodside with Sanderstead. Tenders for the work, described as 'Contract 53' were invited on 15th June 1955 and two months later, on 26th August, the quote submitted by Hugh Brown (Engineers) Ltd of Ashford was officially accepted.

Changes at Addiscombe also included an additional berthing siding and to accommodate this, Platform 3 needed to be demolished. The Chief Civil Engineer contacted the General Manager at Waterloo on 26th April 1956 and provided a list of eight companies who were recommended to undertake the work. On 12th June the contract was awarded to Mears Bros Ltd of Sydenham Road SE26, who quoted £5,481.7s.5d and agreed to complete the task within twenty weeks of the starting date.

Work on the demolition duly started, but with the platform removed, it was found that the foundations of the adjoining screen wall were in extremely poor condition. A new concrete encasement stretching the entire length of the wall at foundation level was therefore added, although of course, this resulted in a price increase. Other problems included changes to the design of a retaining wall which was being constructed beside the carriage shed and the installation of new drainage between sidings 3 and 4, resulting from difficulties arising from wet clay subsoil.

The frontage of Addiscombe station as it appeared soon after the Second World War. It had changed little since completion in 1899, although the wrought ironwork had disappeared, as had the large lamps which once topped the pillars on either side of the forecourt.

Addiscombe – 97

On 24th May 1957, the Chief Civil Engineer informed the General Manager that the changes had been completed, but because of the extra work involved, the final bill exceeded the original quote by £3,881.

The extension of the surviving island platform being carried out by Hugh Brown (Engineers) Ltd also ran into unforeseen difficulties and ended up costing more than previously thought. It now stretched as far as the signal box and, in addition to the alteration of some coal pens in the adjoining yard, a replacement water crane had to be erected to serve the needs of steam locomotives employed on freight duties.

The goods yard, which lay to the west of the formation had opened with the line in 1864, but eventually succumbed to road competition and closed on 17th June 1968.

Seven years earlier, in the summer of 1961, consideration was given to closing the branch to passenger traffic. However, closure of the Woodside-Selsdon route was also under discussion at the same time and it was felt that Addiscombe would serve the needs of passengers who had previously used Bingham Road.

THE FINAL DECLINE

As the years progressed however, passenger loadings went from bad to worse, with even peak services being poorly patronised. The trains, by now formed of 2EPB units, trundled back and forth over the line, but there was little demand for them. At off-peak times it was possible to travel between Elmers End and Addiscombe and not see any other passengers. On arrival at the terminus, there would be no one waiting on the platform and the silence would only be punctuated by the sound of the train's brake compressor.

Those who allowed their imaginations to run into flights of fantasy believed that the adjoining car sheds were haunted, seemingly by a spectral driver from the early days of electrification. Some claimed to have seen him walking around the depot, whilst doors were heard opening and shutting without visible assistance and trains would occasionally start and stop, apparently at their own accord. Be that as it may, there was very little other activity taking place.

By now the station booking office was only open during the morning peak and after that the few passengers had to obtain their tickets from a machine.

From 12th April 1993, drivers ceased booking on at Addiscombe car sheds, but they remained in use for berthing stock. With the demise of the EPBs and their replacement by Networker units however, there was no further need for them, and they eventually closed.

Following the announcement that the line from Elmers End to Woodside was to be incorporated into the Croydon Tramlink scheme it became apparent that the old Addiscombe terminus was to disappear for ever from the railway map of London.

In its final days it was even more desolate than ever. It became totally unstaffed and because of a collapsed ceiling, the main entrance through the booking hall was closed. Passengers wishing to use the station gained access through a small side door at the east end of the frontage and, as no tickets were available, they had to purchase 'Permits to Travel' from a machine on the concourse.

The Mid-Kent Line was extensively re-signalled during the 1970s, but the branch continued with upper quadrant semaphores. There were plans to abolish Addiscombe signal box and operate the route as a single line, but these needed to be implemented earlier than intended when the box was destroyed by fire on the evening of Thursday 7th March 1996. The line remained closed the following day, but reopened on the Saturday with the points clipped at the terminus to allow access to Platform 2 only.

With all traffic now using the former down line, the track on the up side of the branch became overgrown in places and rusty. Members of staff jokingly referred to the service as *'The Two Counties Express'* because it ran non-stop between Kent and Surrey, although in reality the stations concerned had been part of Greater London since 1964.

As closure became imminent a set of edmondson platform tickets were specially printed and delivered to the booking office at Elmers End. These showed the names of Elmers End, Woodside and Addiscombe and were sold as souvenirs.

The last day came on Saturday 31st May 1997 and saw Networker unit No 466016 shuttling back and forth with hand-written commemorative stickers on its cab windows.

The final service train was the 21.40 to Elmers End, which made noisy departures from both branch stations with much sounding of its horn. Soon after, the last train of all, an enthusiasts' special, arrived and departed again. This was marketed as the 'LILO' or 'Last In, Last Out' and was formed of two 4-VEP units. The train had also travelled over the West Croydon - Wimbledon line which had closed for conversion into Tramlink on the same day and carried special headboards at either end.

After closure the station windows were boarded-up and small paper notices were pasted outside advising potential· passengers that the premises were no longer in use. The various signs were removed and the platforms started to submerge beneath a forest of wild foliage, but for a short while there was a vague hope that the buildings might be retained.

The South Eastern & Chatham Railway Society had plans to preserve the old terminus, along with its adjoining car sheds, and establish a working transport museum for south London. Unfortunately this was not to be as the station was completely demolished in June 2001 to provide a site for a residential development.

Right: Addiscombe station seen from its northern end on 29th September 1950, with the signal box in the foreground and part of the goods yard on the right. This had opened with the passenger station and remained in use until 17th June 1968.

Below: A view from the buffer stops at Addiscombe, taken in the 1950s, showing the platform arrangement adopted at the time of rebuilding in 1899. The platforms were originally numbered from east to west, but this was transposed in later years. The steam stock seen on the left is berthed in a siding which lay on the up side. To provide room for an extra siding, the platform on the right, which ended its days as No 3, was demolished in 1956. The painted white bands around the awning pillars were added during the Second World War to improve visibility in the blackout.

Addiscombe – 99

Above: The barrier leading to the island platform at the time when extension and demolition work was under way in 1956-7. It appears that train services had been temporarily suspended, as a chalked notice to the right advises passengers to use buses instead, whilst the poster in the foreground mentions the petrol rationing brought about by the Suez Crisis of 1956.

Left: Looking towards the buffer stops from the island in 1957, after the demolition of Platform 3. The new concrete encasement added at the base of its former rear wall to improve its strength can be seen on the left.

Above: Addiscombe station looking towards the buffer stops in the 1950s or 1960s, with Platform 2 on the left and Platform 1 on the right.

Right: The booking hall in the 1960s, whilst still painted in Southern Railway green and light stone. The doorway onto the concourse can be seen to the right.

Above: The booking hall interior on 7th July 1982, looking towards the entrance doors.

Left: Another view of the booking hall taken at the same date, with the issuing window opposite and the ticket office door marked "Private" on the right.

Right: The booking hall interior, looking towards the doors onto the concourse in July 1982. Comparison with the view reproduced at the bottom of page 107, shows how much brighter it looked after a repaint, although, from the nostalgic point of view, it had perhaps lost much of its character.

Below: Looking across the concourse from its eastern side in July 1982, with the doorway leading into the booking hall just left of centre.

Addiscombe – 103

Above: The concourse from its western side in July 1982, showing the barrier leading to platforms 1 and 2 at centre.

Left: A view taken from the barrier on the same day. Unit 5760 awaits departure from Platform 2, whilst the adjoining siding hosts a train of berthed stock.

104 – London's Disused Railway Stations – Outer South East London

Left: A general view of Addiscombe station as it appeared in July 1982, with both sidings occupied by berthed trains. The characteristic lampposts were a familiar sight around the Southern Railway network and were manufactured in the Company's concrete works at Exmouth Junction.

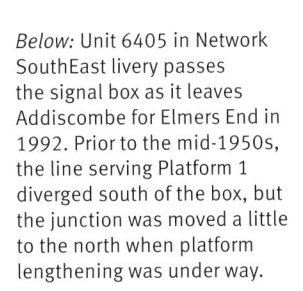

Below: Unit 6405 in Network SouthEast livery passes the signal box as it leaves Addiscombe for Elmers End in 1992. Prior to the mid-1950s, the line serving Platform 1 diverged south of the box, but the junction was moved a little to the north when platform lengthening was under way.

Above: The concourse at Addiscombe as appeared six months after closure.

Left: Looking along the station towards the buffer stops in December 1997, after the nameboards had been removed and the conductor rails partially lifted. Following the signal box fire of March 1996, the points were clipped so all trains arrived at and departed from Platform 2.

106 – London's Disused Railway Stations – Outer South East London

Addiscombe station looking north in December 1997, with the two former berthing sidings on the right.

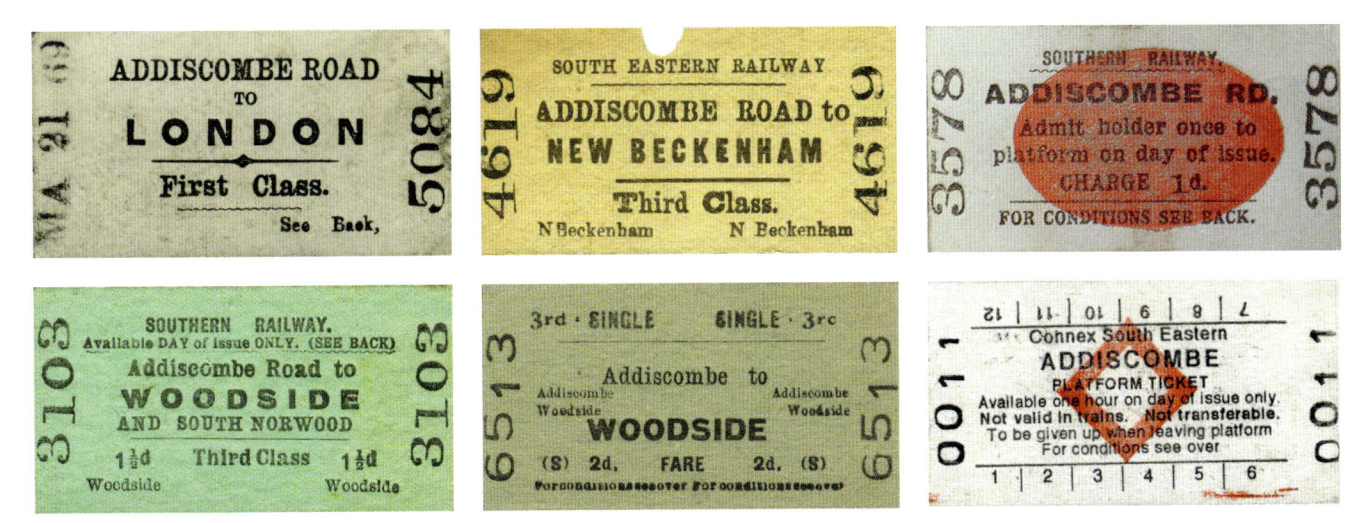

A selection of tickets from Addiscombe: *Top left:* SER First Class single to London issued on 21st March (or May) 1869. *Top centre:* SER Third Class single to New Beckenham issued on 4th July 1888. *Top right:* Southern Railway (SECR style) platform ticket. *Bottom left:* Southern Railway single to Woodside issued 5th August 1923. *Bottom centre:* British Railways Third Class single to Woodside issued on 15th August 1955. *Bottom right:* Souvenir platform ticket produced by Connex South Eastern to commemorate the closing of the station and branch.

Bingham Road

Opened as Bingham Road Halt (Woodside & South Croydon Railway): 1.9.1906.
Closed: (Woodside & South Croydon Railway): 15.3.1915.
Rebuilt and re-opened as Bingham Road (Southern Railway): 30.9.1935.
Closed (British Rail): 16.5.1983.

The down platform at Bingham Road Halt, as it appeared around the early 1930s. It had been constructed largely of old sleepers and cost a little under £103 to build. It is understood that it was originally to be named 'Addiscombe Park', but this was changed to Bingham Road before opening. As can be seen, it was very frugal in nature and was illuminated after dark by oil lamps, which were hung, as required from posts erected along both platforms.

Bingham Road was one of two halts opened on the jointly operated Woodside & South Croydon Railway in 1906, in an attempt to increase passenger revenue. It was located on embankment to the south of Bingham Road, just west of the junction with Northampton Road and comprised two 100ft wooden platforms. Access between these was by means of a boarded crossing and no form of shelter was provided for waiting passengers.

The service was initially provided by SECR steam railmotors, which made sixteen return journeys each day. As no booking facilities were available at either halt, anyone wishing to use them had to buy their ticket from the guard. The line's operation alternated annually between the two companies and during the years when the LBSCR was in charge, a single push-pull coach was provided by one of William Stroudley's *Terrier* 0-6-0Ts. After 1910, this ensemble was replaced by a single class Beyer Peacock railmotor, which had previously been used on the line between Eastbourne and St Leonards.

Unfortunately, the hoped-for traffic never materialised and in 1913, the LBSCR carried out a detailed study of operational costs to evaluate whether it was worth retaining the railmotor service or not. Before any further action could be taken however, the First World War intervened and withdrawal became inevitable. The halts were last used on 14th March 1915 and closed officially the following day. Neither had proved particularly popular, even though Bingham Road was nicely placed as an interchange with the Croydon Corporation Tramway whose Addiscombe terminus was situated nearby.

Above: The Croydon Corporation tram terminus in Lower Addiscombe Road is seen at an unknown date, with the name of the halt prominently displayed on the bridge behind.

The remaining passenger services over the line ceased from the beginning of 1917 and the line entered into a period of semi-disuse. It was occasionally used by excursions and other through workings, but the intermediate stations and halts remained closed.

Spurred on by Colonel H.F. Stephens' proposed Southern Heights Light Railway, which was intended to link Sanderstead with Orpington, the Southern Railway began to consider reopening the line. The track was relaid in 1927, but despite receiving a light railway order at the end of the following year, the Southern Heights scheme failed to materialise. Sadly, Colonel Stephens, a man whose empire of little branches served rural communities, found himself out of his depth. The SR insisted that his new line had to be electrified, but although an offer was made to operate services, the overall cost was beyond the promoter's means. Colonel Stephens never gave up however and was reputedly still trying to raise the necessary capital when he died in Dover on 23rd October 1931.

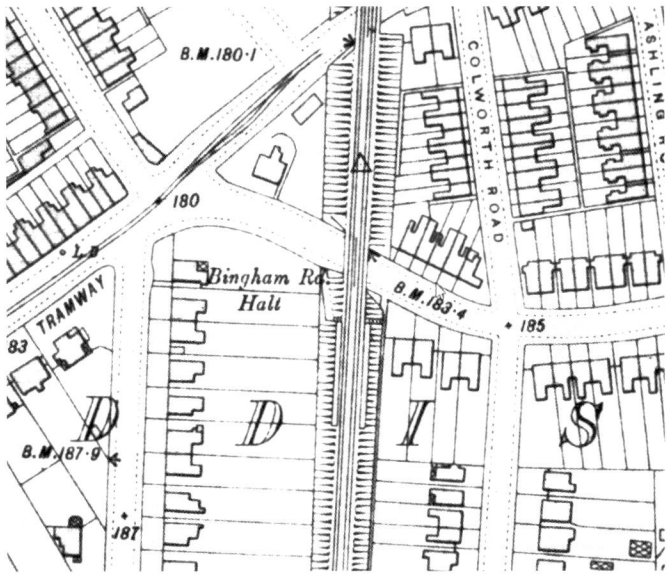

Extract from the Ordnance Survey map of 1910 showing Bingham Road Halt in the centre. North of this stands the bridge featured in the above photograph, whilst the tram terminus appears a little to its left.

Bingham Road – 109

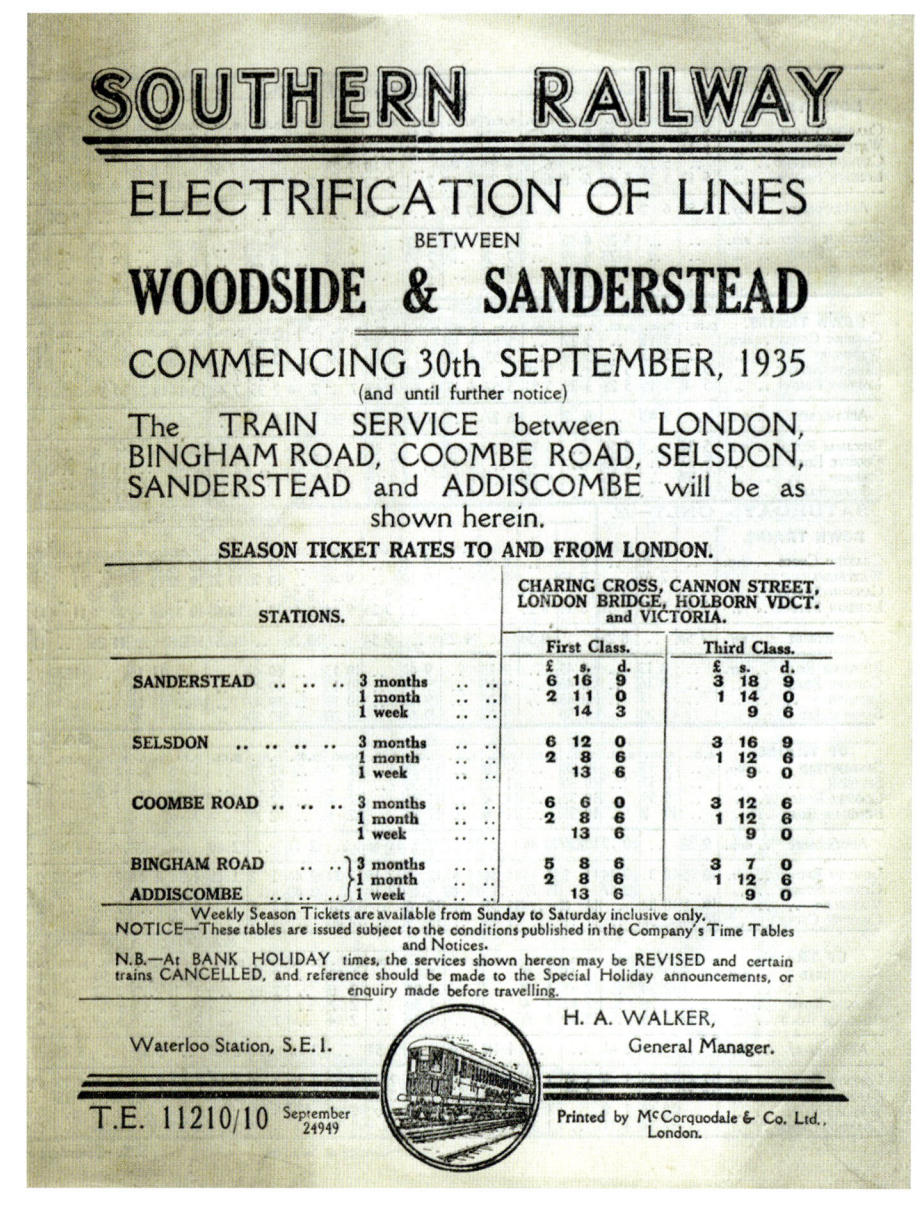

SOUTHERN RAILWAY

ELECTRIFICATION OF LINES
BETWEEN
WOODSIDE & SANDERSTEAD

COMMENCING 30th SEPTEMBER, 1935
(and until further notice)

The TRAIN SERVICE between LONDON, BINGHAM ROAD, COOMBE ROAD, SELSDON, SANDERSTEAD and ADDISCOMBE will be as shown herein.

SEASON TICKET RATES TO AND FROM LONDON.

STATIONS.		CHARING CROSS, CANNON STREET, LONDON BRIDGE, HOLBORN VDCT. and VICTORIA.	
		First Class. £ s. d.	Third Class. £ s. d.
SANDERSTEAD	3 months / 1 month / 1 week	6 16 9 / 2 11 0 / 14 3	3 18 9 / 1 14 0 / 9 6
SELSDON	3 months / 1 month / 1 week	6 12 0 / 2 8 6 / 13 6	3 16 9 / 1 12 6 / 9 0
COOMBE ROAD	3 months / 1 month / 1 week	6 6 0 / 2 8 6 / 13 6	3 12 6 / 1 12 6 / 9 0
BINGHAM ROAD / ADDISCOMBE	3 months / 1 month / 1 week	5 8 6 / 2 8 6 / 13 6	3 7 0 / 1 12 6 / 9 0

Weekly Season Tickets are available from Sunday to Saturday inclusive only.
NOTICE—These tables are issued subject to the conditions published in the Company's Time Tables and Notices.
N.B.—At BANK HOLIDAY times, the services shown hereon may be REVISED and certain trains CANCELLED, and reference should be made to the Special Holiday announcements, or enquiry made before travelling.

Waterloo Station, S.E.1.
H. A. WALKER, General Manager.

T.E. 11210/10 September 24949
Printed by McCorquodale & Co. Ltd., London.

Above: Undated Woodside & South Croydon Joint Line railmotor ticket.

Below: Bingham Road Halt looking north at an unknown date.

Left: Handbill produced by the Southern Railway, announcing the electrification of the former Woodside & South Croydon Joint Line and the introduction of new services from 30th September 1935.

Despite having appeared briefly on certain Southern Railway route maps, the proposed light railway faded into obscurity, but the plan to electrify the former WSCR and the continuation to Sanderstead eventually became a reality.

As part of the scheme, announced in 1934, the disused halt at Bingham Road would be demolished and replaced by a new station at a cost of £10,000. Work on rehabilitating the line duly started and it was ready for inspection by the Ministry of Transport in the autumn of 1935.

In his report dated 2nd October 1935, Colonel A.C. Trench described the route as being 3miles 17chains in length and *"presently used by a comparatively small amount of steam traffic."* He stated that *"the electric supply is fed from existing third rail at Woodside as far as Bingham Road station, where there are switches normally open; on the south side of these switches, the third rails are fed from a new sub-station at South Croydon which contains 2,000KW rectifiers and feeds at Selsdon, the substation being controlled from Norwood."* He went on to say *"An old halt at Bingham Road is being reconstructed as a station; construction is not yet complete, but I was assured by the Engineer that it would be sufficiently advanced by Monday September 30th, for convenient and safe use by passengers; I see no reason why this should not be so, provided that steps are taken to keep the passengers, who will presumably be small in number at first, to the portion of the platform on which the workmen are not working overhead, and I was assured that steps would be taken to safeguard this point."*

Bingham Road station sported some fine 1930s running-in nameboards well into the British Rail Corporate Image era, as is evident from this view taken from its northern end in the 1970s.

He recorded that when finished the platforms would stretch to a length of 520ft and would *"be provided with waiting rooms and conveniences as well as a booking office."* At the time of his inspection, the installation of electric lighting had not been completed, so the new station had to be temporarily lit by oil lamps.

Bingham Road had brick-built entrances on both sides of the line, from which covered stairways ascended to the concrete platforms. The buildings were wooden and incorporated glazed awnings of a style then favoured by the SR.

The line re-opened on 30th September 1935, a few days before Colonel Trench wrote his report, and was provided with a half-hourly service linking Sanderstead with Charing Cross or Cannon Street. Trains were increased to three an hour during the peak periods, but were never filled to capacity. Unfortunately the stations were in areas already well served, with Bingham Road being close to the former Mid-Kent Railway terminus at Addiscombe.

From the outset, passenger receipts were disappointing and the advent of the Second World War in 1939 didn't exactly help matters. From 16th October that year, the Monday to Friday off-peak frequency was cut back to one an hour, and the service ceased after 7pm. At the same time, Saturday trains ceased running after 3pm and the line was closed on Sundays. An attempt to return to pre-war frequencies was made after the end of hostilities, but there was no real demand and reductions became inevitable. From 26th September 1949, the off-peak through trains to and from central London were withdrawn and replaced by half-hourly shuttles which rattled back and forth between Sanderstead and Elmers End, where they connected with trains on the Charing Cross-Hayes route. This did little to improve the line's popularity and further cuts were deemed necessary ten years later. Despite the decline in usage the route was included in a mid-l950s scheme to lengthen platforms so that they could accommodate ten-car trains. Bingham Road had its platforms extended at the southern ends and, at the same time, had remedial work carried out on its drainage.

From 2nd November 1959, Monday-Friday services ceased operation between 10.45am and 3.15pm and stopped completely after 8.45pm, whilst there were no trains on Saturdays after 3.45pm.

In 1960 Bingham Road was used in the comedy film *The Rebel* starring the late lamented Tony Hancock. For this it was disguised as a fictitious station called *'Fortune Green South'* and had its nameboards temporarily altered accordingly. In the opening scene, the up side is totally crowded with waiting commuters, whilst only one person, the character played by Hancock, is on the other. Two green liveried Southern EPB units draw up at the platforms at exactly the same time and Hancock leaps onto one, dashes through the compartment, then by opening the off-side doors gets into the up train before the burgeoning crowds. Unfortunately, the station was never to know such patronage in reality.

By the summer of 1961, BR was actively seeking to close the line completely, leaving just a short stretch at its southern end to serve Selsdon goods yard. Consideration was also being given to withdrawing services over the Addiscombe branch, but a letter written on 13th August that year by the Line Traffic Manager, Essex House, Croydon, complained that if both closures took place they would put an undue strain on stations within his district, particularly East Croydon and Norwood Junction. Others clearly shared the same opinion, so Addiscombe was dropped from the scheme, leaving just the Woodside - Selsdon line under threat.

An investigation into the route began in August 1962 and as expected it proved uneconomic to operate. The annual branch traffic receipts were quoted as £9,005, of which £7,349 came from the sale of season tickets. The issue of other types of tickets amounted to £1,631, which together with £19 described as *"miscellaneous"* and a meagre £6 earned from parcels traffic, accounted for the remainder. Traffic was light, with just twenty-three trains in each direction on weekdays and sixteen each way on Saturdays.

At the time Bingham Road was staffed by a Senior Porter, an Acting Senior Porter and a Junior Porter. It was described as being the busiest station on the line, but being just 58chains by rail from Woodside and 700 yards walk from Addiscombe, it was deemed expendable. Externally at least, the station appeared to be in good condition, but it was suggested that around £6,200 would need to be spent over the next five years if it was to be kept in an acceptable state of repair.

Following meetings with Sectional Council members at Waterloo on 12th September 1962, it was agreed to go ahead with the scheme. Closure notices began to appear three months later on 14th December, announcing a

The station retained its characteristic Southern Railway 'target' name tablets for many years. These dated from 1935.

withdrawal date of 4th March 1963, but objections resulted in this being delayed. One of the local MPs was the then Minister of Transport, Ernest Marples, who felt that the closure would result in commuters facing hardships as it was not practical at the time to provide adequate replacement 'bus services.

On 18th December 1963, the line officially won a three year reprieve, although it was stated that the situation would be reviewed after three years. Five days later BR arranged for advertisements announcing the reprieve to appear in the *Croydon Times* and *Croydon Advertiser* and replaced the closure notices with new posters stating that the route would remain open. After the three-year period elapsed additional cuts were implemented, but still the line soldiered on.

From 2nd January 1967, the Saturday peak-hour shuttles were withdrawn and re-routed to serve Addiscombe instead. Then, later in the year, from 10th July, the weekday service was further reduced, with no trains running between 9.50am and 4.17pm.

Following the withdrawal of the remaining through workings to central London in April 1976, the scene was set for final closure. This came in May 1983, by which time the route had taken on the inevitable run-down appearance.

Bingham Road was staffed until closure, with a booking office at the London end of the up platform. This was manned during traffic hours by a single clerk supplied by Addiscombe, but for the rest of the day there was no-one in attendance.

Following closure the track was soon removed and by March 1984, the wooden buildings at Bingham Road had been vandalised. Broken glass lay on the concrete platforms, and the booking office, which a year before had been stocked with edmondson tickets, lay open with the door wrenched from its hinges. The inevitable demolition followed, leaving just a few scant remains at street level. The up side entrance continued to be recognisable, with its mangled folding gate lying amidst the rubble and weeds, but the bridge which once carried the tracks above the road had gone completely.

The embankment which had previously accommodated the platforms survived for a while, but eventually this was removed during the construction of Croydon Tramlink. The first part of the new system opened on Wednesday 10th May 2000, when trams began running between central Croydon and New Addington. A fortnight later, on Tuesday 23rd May, the section to Beckenham Junction was brought into public use and this follows the old WSCR route through Bingham Road. The formation is no longer elevated however and Bingham Road is crossed on the level immediately south of the present Addiscombe tram stop. A solitary section of broken wall which once formed part of the old up side entrance was still standing in April 2003, but apart from that, Bingham Road station had disappeared completely.

Looking south along the down platform at Bingham Road during the 1970s, with a Southern Railway running-in nameboard prominent on the left.

Above: Another Southern Railway running-in board survived towards the southern end of the up platform, although by the time this photograph was taken in the 1970s, its lower parts had been partially eaten away by rust.

Left: A view from the northern end of the down platform, looking towards Woodside at around the same time.

114 – London's Disused Railway Stations – Outer South East London

Above: The down side station entrance and adjoining bridge above the street in the 1970s.

Right: An unusual view, taken from the cab of an approaching train, with the later platform extensions seen in the foreground. Although Southern Railway signage was retained towards the station's northern end, the newer extensions were provided with BR style nameboards, including totems which were fixed to the concrete lampposts.

Bingham Road – 115

Above: A down train formed of a 2-EPB unit enters Bingham Road in the 1970s.

Right: The station viewed from street level in February 1980, with its up side entrance visible on the left.

Bingham Road station on 30th December 1980.

Upper left: The up side stairs looking towards the booking office.

Upper right: The booking office, with its ticket-issuing window to the left of centre.

Right: The former down side booking office.

Below: The down side entrance with its stairway link to the platform above.

Above: The up side entrance on 14th April 1983. By this time the station was beginning to look rather run-down.

Right: The down side entrance, recorded on the same date.

Above: A selection of tickets: *Top left:* SECR single from Selsdon Road issued on 1st January 1910. *Top right:* SR 3rd Class single to Clock House issued on 11th December 1945. *Bottom left:* BTC platform ticket issued on 4th May 1958. *Bottom right:* British Railways 2nd Class single to Coombe Road issued on 31st May 1961.

118 – London's Disused Railway Stations – Outer South East London

Above: The exterior of the waiting room, which was located on the up side at Bingham Road in December 1980. The door closest to the camera provided staff access to the ticket office.

Right: The interior of the waiting room, photographed on the same date, showing the benches, which were very much in the style of the mid-1930s, with a hint of art deco.

Above: Bingham Road station looking towards Coombe Road in April 1983, with the staff doorway serving the erstwhile down side ticket office beneath the 'Way Out' sign on the left.

Left: With closure looming, the station started to be targetted by graffiti vandals. This view was taken in May 1983, looking from the top of the up side stairs towards the platforms. The surviving ticket office was out of shot to the right of the photograph.

Above: The track remained in situ for a while after closure, including the conductor rails, but all through the station had been lifted by March 1984, when this photograph was taken. As can be seen, Bingham Road had suffered vandalism and the former ticket office had been damaged by fire.

Right: The interior of the station waiting room, viewed on the same occasion. The nice 1930s benches had long gone by this time, although whether these were scrapped or found use elsewhere is not known.

Above and below: The disused Bingham Road station looking north in March 1984. Although most of the track had gone by this date, a stretch of up line survived and can be seen beyond the platforms.

After standing derelict for a short while, Bingham Road station was demolished during 1984. This view shows the down side staircase whilst work was under way.

By the autumn of 1984, the former station had been largely reduced to rubble. This view looks north and includes the up platform ramp alongside the permanent way hut on the left.

Here we see the site of the station, as it appeared in July 2019, with the lines of Croydon Tramlink crossing the road on the left. To the right of these, a broken brick wall was all that remained of the up side entrance. This photograph makes an interesting comparison with the view reproduced at the bottom of page 116.

Bingham Road – 123

Coombe Road

Opened as Coombe Lane (Woodside & South Croydon Railway): 10.8.1885.
Closed: (Woodside & South Croydon Railway): 1.1.1917.
Rebuilt and re-opened as Coombe Road (Southern Railway): 30.9.1935.
Closed (British Rail): 16.5.1983.

Coombe Lane station, looking towards Woodside from the up platform at an unknown date prior to 1917. Tubs of flowering plants adorn the base of the canopy columns, whilst in the distance can be seen the southernmost of three contiguous tunnels, which are now part of the Croydon Tramlink system.

The 2mile 29.71chain Woodside & South Croydon Railway was authorised in 1880 and was worked as a joint venture by the SER and LBSCR under an agreement dated 10th August 1882. It diverged from the South Eastern 12chains south of Woodside station and skirted Croydon before reaching a junction with the Oxted line at Selsdon Road. At the time of opening in 1885, the only intermediate station was situated at Coombe Lane, 53chains north of Selsdon Road. This comprised two platforms, with substantial buildings constructed in yellow stock brick and wood. A signal box, initially equipped with six working and two spare levers, was provided at the south end of the up side, but there was no goods yard, as this was forbidden by the authorising Act at the insistence of a local landowner.

When inspected by Major General Hutchinson on behalf of the Board of Trade in October 1884, he reported that the station still required platform ramps and refinements to its signalling, but was seemingly otherwise complete. He was dissatisfied with other sections of the route however, so its opening was delayed for a number of months until these were remedied.

Class Q1 0-4-4T No 141 approaches Coombe Lane from the Woodside direction in SECR days.

Above: The south end of Coombe Lane station in the early years of the twentieth century, showing the signal box which adjoined the up platform.

Right: An SECR steam railcar, thought to be No 4, enters Coombe Lane station some time after 1906.
No 4 was the usual railcar seen on this line and was based at Bricklayer's Arms. Her working day started with the 6.17am service from New Cross to Addiscombe Road and ended with the 9.00pm from Addiscombe Road to New Cross, but she otherwise shuttled back and forth between Woodside and Selsdon Road. When unavailable she was replaced on this duty by No 3 or No 7, which were both shedded at Tonbridge.

Coombe Road – 125

Although available for through running, the majority of trains operated only between Selsdon Road and a bay platform at Woodside. Regular through workings remained very few and far between, although it was often used as a relief route for excursion traffic. Apart from this, occasional freight trains trundled through, although these never called en-route due to the lack of intermediate goods yards.

At first the area served by the line was semi-rural, but by the beginning of the twentieth century urbanisation was beginning to spread. In an attempt to create extra traffic a pair of halts were subsequently added, including that already described at Bingham Road, and a railmotor service was introduced. This failed to improve the route's fortunes however and ceased in March 1915. The remaining service, although poorly patronised, survived until 1st January 1917, when all passenger trains were withdrawn and Coombe Lane station was closed.

Extract from the 1932 Ordnance Survey map, showing Coombe Lane station during its first period of closure.

Below: Coombe Lane station, looking towards Woodside after closure, possibly around 1921. As can be seen, the platform lamps had been partially dismantled, but otherwise it appears to have remained largely intact.

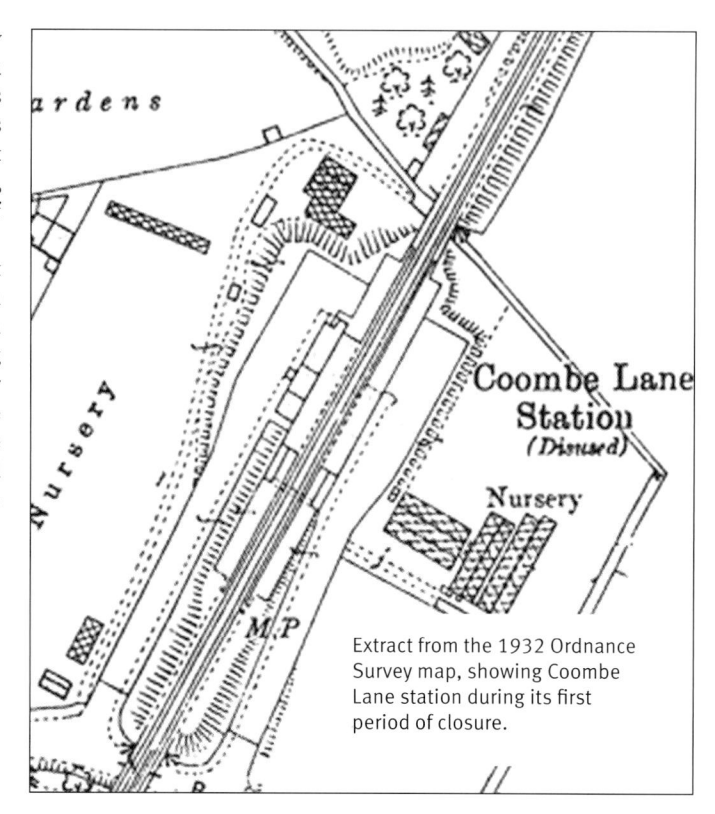

There then followed a period when the W&SCR saw little traffic, although it continued to be used by through excursions and hop-pickers' specials. In addition to these, the odd goods train still ran, together with a few empty stock workings, but the local service was not restored and the erstwhile passenger facilities remained abandoned. Occasionally an article would appear in the local press, suggesting that the line should be reopened to passengers, but despite extensive track renewal in 1927, this did not happen.

However in 1934, the Southern Railway surprisingly announced that it would be electrified and again provided with a full passenger service, although the General Manager was seemingly sceptical about its prospects.

Nevertheless the project went ahead and the derelict station at Coombe Lane was rebuilt for around £7,200. The old buildings were demolished and the platforms extended to a length of 520ft, although the work was still incomplete when inspected by Col. A.C. Trench on behalf of the Ministry of Transport. His report, dated 2nd October 1935 mentioned that temporary lighting was being *"provided by oil lamps pending the installation of electric light"*, but he felt that *"no appreciable inconvenience should be caused to passengers by the progress of the works."*

In its new form, Coombe Lane was renamed Coombe Road, and boasted modern red-brick buildings. Most of its earlier structures had been swept away, although parts of the stairways remained original.

Sadly, even in its electrified form, the line failed to attract a great deal of patronage, largely because it was located close to other routes with well-established services. Nevertheless in May 1956 the platforms were extended by the firm of Hugh Brown (Engineers) at their northern ends to accommodate 10-car trains, although this was undoubtedly an unnecessary exercise.

The early 1960s closure proposal, which has been detailed in the Bingham Road section, suggested that as Coombe Road was only 900 yards walk from South Croydon, passengers would only suffer minor inconvenience if services were withdrawn. At the time the station was staffed by two Leading Porters and appeared to be in good condition, although a report suggested that repairs estimated at £6,300 would prove necessary within five years.

Closure was proposed for 4th March 1963 but the line won a reprieve and was retained. Coombe Road remained staffed, but the down side buildings were subsequently demolished, presumably to save on repair bills. That on the up side was left standing however and continued to house the booking office. Weeds were springing up through the platform surfaces and some of the 1930s-style lamp shades were reduced to their skeletal metal, having had their glass destroyed by vandals.

Patronage of the line went from bad to worse and its closure became inevitable. At the end there were nine up trains in the morning, all originating from Sanderstead

The disused Coombe Lane station looking towards Selsdon Road sometime around 1927.

except one, which started from Selsdon at 8.57am. Seven trains ran in the opposite direction, one of which terminated at Selsdon to form the service mentioned above. In the evening there were ten trains each way calling at all stations, although one of these, the 6.50pm ex-Sanderstead ran fast from Selsdon to Elmers End.

Even on the very last day of passenger services, the line was scarcely crowded, although a fair number turned up to travel on the final working, the 7.30pm from Sanderstead to Elmers End. By March 1984, the track from Woodside Junction to near Spencer Road had been lifted and demolition work at Coombe Road had just commenced, in readiness for houses to be built on the site. Within a short time the station had disappeared and redevelopment commenced, but this was not to be the end however, as the trackbed was subsequently incorporated into the Croydon Tramway network.

The first section of this to be brought into public use was that linking central Croydon with New Addington. This opened on Wednesday 10th May 2000 and utilises part of the old line after diverging from the Beckenham Junction route at Sandilands. Immediately east of Sandilands, trams travelling towards New Addington curve to the south then reach a succession of three adjoining tunnels built for the W&SCR. One continuous tunnel may have been more desirable, but the nature of the terrain meant that the central section had to be built by the cut-and-cover-method. The most northerly part was known as Woodside Tunnel and stretches for 266yds. This is followed by the 122yd Park Hill Tunnel and finally the 157yd Coombe Lane Tunnel.

Having emerged from the southernmost portal, trams continue for a short distance before reaching the site of Coombe Road station, which has vanished without trace. Beyond here the old line continued on embankment towards Selsdon Road, but the trams diverge eastwards onto a purpose-built formation towards the stop at Lloyd Park. It seems that having led an unsuccessful career for most of its existence, part of the old Woodside & South Croydon Railway had at long last found success and has a place in the London of the twenty-first century.

Above: Exterior of the main up side building at Coombe Road, as it appeared after its 1935 rebuilding. The photograph was taken some time after nationalisation, although some fine Southern Railway lettering survived above the entrance door.

Left: A general view of the station, looking towards the mouth of Coombe Lane Tunnel from the down platform during the first half of the 1950s, with an SR running-in board on the left.

Above: Looking north from the up platform in the 1950s, with a train approaching from the Woodside end.

Right: Here we see work under way on lengthening the northern end of the down platform in May 1956.

Coombe Road – 129

Above: Looking north from a little beyond the down platform ramp, possibly in the 1970s, with a British Railways white-on-green running-in board on the left.

Left: An ex-Southern Railway target-style name tablet.

Left: A British Railways totem lamp tablet, photographed at the same time. These were placed on the 1956 platform extensions, whilst the old Southern targets were retained elsewhere.

Left: A view from inside the station entrance in 1980, with the barrier leading to the up platform to the left and the ticket office staff doorway to the right of centre.

Below (left): Although the station was rebuilt in 1935, the stairways retained their original walls as seen here.

Below (right): Another feature that remained largely unaltered from the station's Coombe Lane days was the passenger subway linking the two platforms. This photograph dates from 1980.

Coombe Road – 131

Right: The up platform building as it appeared in 1980, after the station had been re-signed in the corporate British Rail style with black lettering on white boards.

Left: A view taken from beneath the up side canopy, looking south in 1980. The bench seats on the left were clearly intended for platform use, but those on the right were presumably once located inside a waiting room and appear to have deteriorated slightly in an outdoor environment. In the medium distance can be seen the top of the stairway, whilst at centre is the ticket office issuing window. This office retained traditional Edmondson tickets until closure, although latterly its stocks were limited.

Right: As previously mentioned, the buildings protecting the stairway tops retained much of their original brickwork, although they both received glazing and new roofs when the station was rebuilt in the 1930s. This view looks towards the down side.

Right: The station entrance as it appeared in 1983, shortly before closure.

Below: Another view from 1983. This time looking north from the down platform, with the southern portal of Coombe Lane Tunnel just visible in the distance.

Coombe Road – 133

Above: A train approaches the up platform at Coombe Road in May 1983, shortly before closure. The length of plain wall opposite marks the site of the former down side building, whilst an empty frame alongside the second lamp post on the left shows that at least one of the station nameboards had already been removed.

Left: A pair of 2-EPBs, led by unit No 5746, pause at Coombe Road's down platform in May 1983.

Above: The up side building basks in the morning sunshine on its final day of use, 13th May 1983.

Right: A 2-EPB unit pauses at the up platform whilst working a service to Elmers End on Friday 13th May 1983.

Coombe Road – 135

Above: As the final day wore on, enthusiasts began to gather along the route. Here some small groups of them can be seen at Coombe Road, as an afternoon train pulls in from Elmers End.

Below: A sign at the base of the station approach, showing its opening times.

Far right: An up train passes over the bridge at the south end of the station in 1983.

136 – London's Disused Railway Stations – Outer South East London

Right: By March 1984, the land adjoining the main building had been cleared so that the demolition gang could move in. The building itself remained intact at the time, but its days were now numbered.

Below: Here we see the platform side of the building as it appeared on the same occasion. A rather battered notice advising trespassers not to step on the electrified track can be seen propped up at centre, despite the track having already been lifted. The section of platform in the right foreground had been partly demolished so that demolition vehicles could access the formation.

Coombe Road – 137

Spencer Road Halt

Opened: (Woodside & South Croydon Railway): 1.9.1906.
Closed: (Woodside & South Croydon Railway): 15.3.1915.

This simple wooden halt was located to the west of Spencer Road, between Coombe Lane and Selsdon Road on the Woodside & South Croydon Joint Railway. It comprised two 100ft platforms, but there were no buildings and tickets had to be purchased on the train from the conductor-guard.

By opening halts at Spencer Road and Bingham Road and providing a steam railmotor service, it was hoped to increase the profitability of the line, but unfortunately this was not to be. The railmotors were taken off the route after the close of traffic on 14th March 1915 and both halts fell into disuse. As mentioned earlier, the line itself remained open for other trains for a little longer, but eventually succumbed to the inevitable on 1st January 1917.

From then on the Woodside & South Croydon line saw very little in the way of trains, although it was sometimes used as a relief route for excursion traffic. Apart from this, occasional freight trains trundled through, although these never called en-route because there were no intermediate goods yards. During the 1920s the line continued to appear on certain Southern Railway route maps, complete with its stations and halts, but it remained closed to regular passenger traffic.

The modernisation scheme of the 1930s resulted in regular services being reinstated, but Spencer Road, remained disused. The actual date of demolition is uncertain, but it was probably around the time that electrification work was under way.

At its northern end, a footbridge formed part of a footpath between Spencer Road and Birdhurst Rise and this still survives. This was erected as part of a pedestrian route, although wooden gates at the base of its stairways provided access to the platforms.

Above: Ex-South Eastern Railway E class 4-4-0 No A175 passes the disused halt at Spencer Road on 13th September 1933, with an excursion train bound for Hastings. At the rear of the platforms can be seen wooden posts which had previously accommodated oil lamps.

Left: SECR Third Class single from Selsdon Road to Spencer Road Halt issued on 24th November 1906.

Right: Extract from the 1:2500 Ordnance Survey map of 1912, showing the halt at centre, along with the footpaths which provided access from both Spencer Road and Birdhurst Rise. The footbridge over the line was for general pedestrian use, but also served gates which led to the platforms.

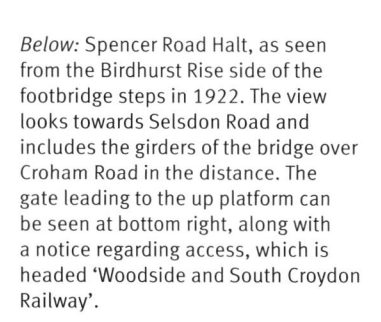

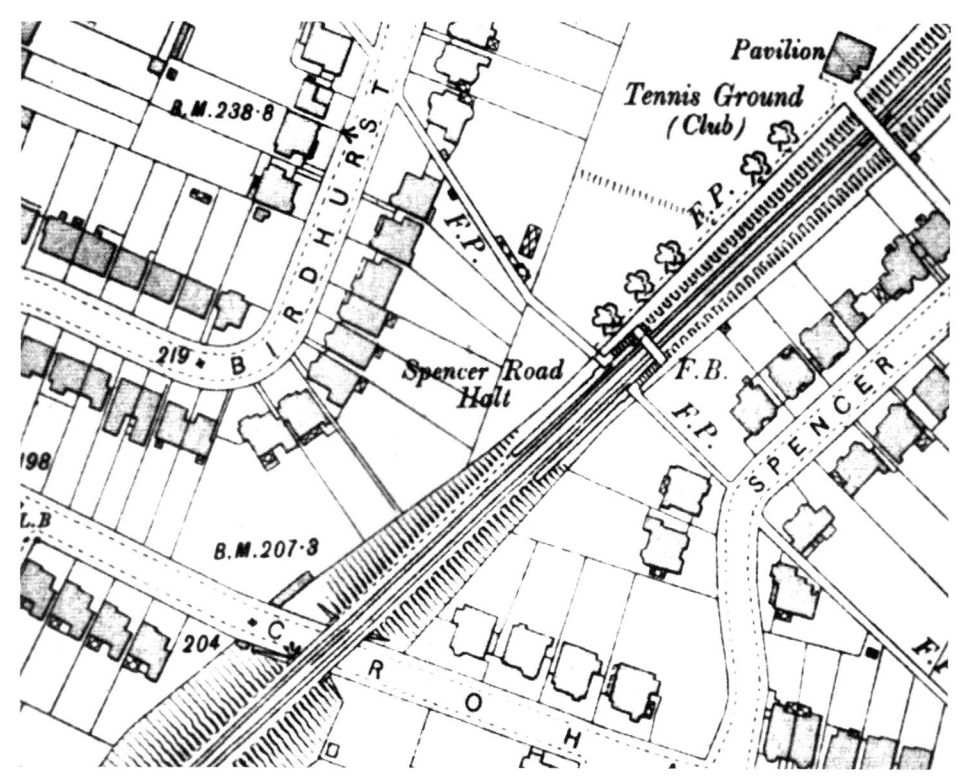

Below: Spencer Road Halt, as seen from the Birdhurst Rise side of the footbridge steps in 1922. The view looks towards Selsdon Road and includes the girders of the bridge over Croham Road in the distance. The gate leading to the up platform can be seen at bottom right, along with a notice regarding access, which is headed 'Woodside and South Croydon Railway'.

Spencer Road Halt – 139

Left: The up side of the halt, viewed from the footbridge steps on the Spencer Road side. A further Woodside and South Croydon Railway notice can be seen at bottom left, and the wooden oil-lamp posts stand out nicely behind the platform fencing.

Left: An F1 4-4-0 passes Spencer Road on an up through train at an unknown date.

Below: Two-car electric unit No 5725 is seen passing the site of the halt as it heads beneath the footbridge on its journey to Elmers End on 13th May 1985.

Above: The site of Spencer Road Halt, looking towards Woodside on 8th October 1991. Although the majority of branch track had been lifted in the previous decade, some had been retained at its southern end to serve an oil depot at Selsdon.

Right: The site as seen from the footbridge on 3rd July 2019, with rusting remnants of track just about visible in the foreground.

Spencer Road Halt – 141

Selsdon

Opened as Selsdon Road (London Brighton & South Coast and South Eastern Railways): 1885.
Temporarily closed (London Brighton & South Coast and South Eastern and Chatham Railways): 1.1.1917.
Oxted line platforms reopened: 1.3.1919.
Woodside line platforms reopened and station renamed Selsdon (Southern Railway): 30.9.1935.
Oxted line platforms closed (British Railways Southern Region): 14.6.1959.
Station completely closed (British Rail Southern Region): 16.5.1983.

Selsdon Road station was located at the junction of the Woodside & South Croydon and Oxted lines and comprised four platform faces. The up WSCR platform was joined to that serving the down Oxted line at its southern end, although the levels of both were slightly different. This was emphasised by the change in height displayed by the attendant awnings and resulted in the need of a short flight of steps descending from the WSCR side for passengers wishing to transfer from one to the other. The main building was located towards the station's northern end and was accessed by a sloping approach which continued from the south end of Moreton Road. This building, which, like others provided at the station, was largely built of wood, lay between the two diverging routes and accommodated the booking office. A footbridge was erected to link the two Oxted platforms, but the pair serving the WSCR were linked by subway. A small goods yard was provided from the outset and lay to the east of the passenger station. Access to this was from the Woodside direction and was served by a cabin known as 'Selsdon Road North'. This was located west of the line and stood a short distance beyond the Woodside end of the up platform. Another cabin, 'Selsdon Road Junction', stood immediately south of the up Oxted platform and controlled movements over the junction between the two routes.

The station was largely complete by October 1884 when it was inspected on behalf of the Board of Trade by Major General Hutchinson. However, problems elsewhere on the WSCR, mainly at Woodside, resulted in its opening being delayed. At the time of inspection, a Selsdon Road signal box was recorded as having nine working levers and four spare, but unfortunately the report does not specify which cabin was referred to. Major General Hutchinson required some signalling refinements to be carried out along with a few minor station alterations, but unfortunately the writing on his inspection report is difficult to read, so details are scant. It seems however that at least one platform initially ended with steps, instead of a ramp and this needed to be changed before the premises were deemed ready for use.

Major General Hutchinson made two further visits to the WSC line and on 27th July 1885 he agreed that it was ready for opening. Traffic commenced on 10th August

Notice dated 28th December 1885 stating that the station had been brought into use and listing sample costs of season tickets. Caterham Junction referred to near the base of the bill was renamed Purley on 1st October 1888.

1885 and Selsdon Road station presumably opened at the same time, although the London railway historian H.V. Borley only recorded an opening date of "1885".

The premises closed at the beginning of 1917 when the service from Woodside was withdrawn, but the Oxted line platforms were brought back into use on 1st March 1919. The other pair remained closed however and were not re-opened until electrification in 1935. Unlike the other WSCR stations, Selsdon Road was little altered, although the down platform had to be lengthened to 520ft and a certain amount of re-surfacing work needed to be done.

With the introduction of electric services over the Woodside route, the entire station reverted to public use and its name was shortened to 'Selsdon'. As the re-opening became imminent it was decided that there was no further use for Selsdon Road North signal box, so this was abolished in September 1935 and operation of the goods yard transferred to the junction cabin. This box was recorded in 1920 as having an 1883 brick base covering a ground area of 18ft 1in x 11ft and a height above rail level of 5ft 9ins. It was re-locked in 1904 when its frame comprised twenty-four working levers and none spare. At the same time Selsdon Road North was equipped with twenty-one levers, of which one was spare.

The station remained completely operative throughout the Second World War and into the 1950s, but by this time it was beginning to appear rather run down. Weeds sprang up beside the approach road and the wooden buildings looked neglected. The Oxted platforms, latterly provided with a meagre service, were taken out of use from 14th June 1959.

Extract from the 1:2500 Ordnance Survey map of 1913, showing the station at centre.
Passengers could access the platforms from either end by means of two inclined approaches. That to the south served Selsdon Road itself, whilst that to the north led by way of Moreton Road to Croham Road.
No detailed plans of the station have been located but, from evidence available it seems that there was only one booking office. This was located towards the Croham Road end and stood in the vee formed by the diverging platforms 2 and 3. Passengers entering from the south did so by way of a gate onto the down Woodside platform, then headed for the booking office by using the subway.
The goods yard lay to the east of the passenger station and access to this was controlled by Selsdon Road North signal box. which appears towards the top of the map. The other cabin, Selsdon Road Junction, was located by the south end of the up Oxted platform.
The tracks seen on the extreme left are part of the LBSCR main line linking London with Brighton and other South Coast destinations.

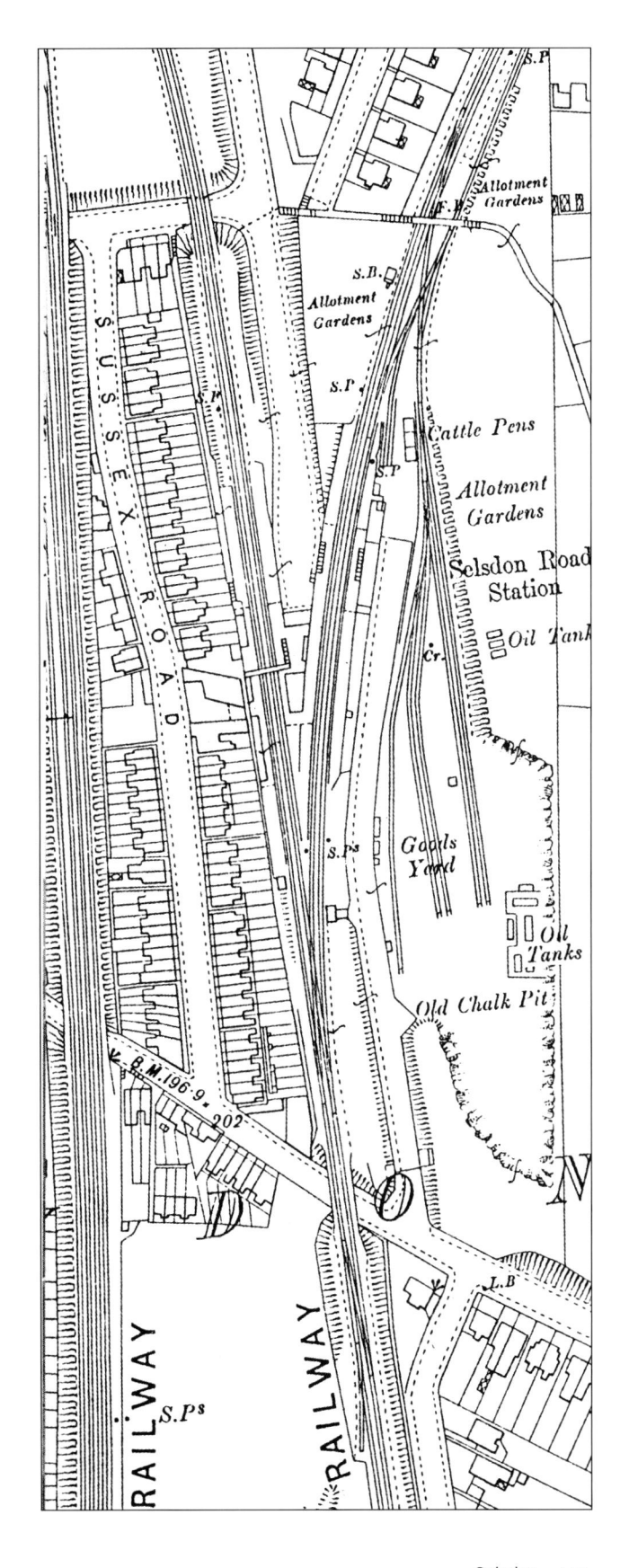

Complete closure was threatened in the early 1960s, when the Woodside line was declared uneconomical to operate, but it was subsequently reprieved. The proposal envisaged the end of all former WSCR services and the lifting of track along most of the route. The only exception being from a point 400yds north of Selsdon No 5 shunt signal, which would be retained in connection with the goods yard. The report, which was dated 5th September 1962, also stated that an estimated £4,800 would be required over a five year period to keep the premises in a good state of repair. This emphasised however that the finance would be required for the buildings on *"the Mid-Kent"* side, as those which had served the Oxted line were presumably due for demolition.

Interestingly, the report makes no mention of station staff being employed at Selsdon, so the turns were possibly covered from elsewhere. The only employees referred to were a pair of Class 3 signalmen who would have been retained despite closure of the Woodside branch, as the box was required to control the goods yard.

The actual dates when the station buildings were demolished are uncertain, but work probably started around 1963. By 1966 there were only short sections of replacement canopy above the stairwell entrances and a newly erected ticket hut, reminiscent of a garden shed, on the down side. Both canopy sections remained standing until 12th November 1977 when that on the down side was blown down in a gale, and the other was removed later in the month.

All that now remained were the bare empty platforms, with those still in use looking little better than the pair which had closed. Tickets were nominally available from the wooden hut, but this was scarcely, if ever, staffed in later years. Selsdon remained gas-lit until the end with its unattended mantles burning night and day. It was one of the last, if not the very last station within Greater London to be illuminated in this manner.

Complete closure came with the end of the Woodside & South Croydon line on 16th May 1983, after which the fittings were removed. The route had possessed an air of desolation for some time, and nowhere was this more apparent than at Selsdon. It was a depressing but unforgettable experience to stand on the deserted station as night descended, with only the popping of the gas lamps to break the silence.

After closure, the former WSCR side became very overgrown with the erstwhile up platform being partly demolished, but those which once served the Oxted line were left mainly untouched.

The Junction signal box remained in use until 1st April, 1984 when it was abolished. The goods yard had ceased to deal with general traffic on 7th October 1968, but was partially retained to serve an oil depot until March 1993.

Wainwright C Class 0-6-0 No 90, resplendent in her livery of SECR lined green, stands by Selsdon Road North signal box in pre-grouping days, with the public footbridge linking Whitmead Road with Dornton Road seen on the right.

144 – London's Disused Railway Stations – Outer South East London

Stroudley Class A1 *Terrier* No 70 *Poplar* stands beside Selsdon North box with a typical LBSCR suburban train used on the Woodside line before the introduction of railmotors.

No 70 was one of her class to be named after stations of the London & Blackwall Railway, which LBSCR passengers could reach by changing off the East London Line at Shadwell. The others were: 38 *Millwall*, 55 *Stepney*, 72 *Fenchurch*, 74 *Shadwell*, 75 *Blackwall* and 79 *Minories*. The last mentioned is a bit of a puzzle as the A1s were not introduced until 1872, but Minories station closed in 1853. Happily Nos 55, 70 and 72 have been preserved.

The Oxted line platforms looking south in 1921, with part of the building containing the booking office visible on the left.

Above: The Woodside line platforms at Selsdon Road, looking towards the junction in 1921, with the booking office building just visible behind the lady on the right. This side of the station was out of use at the time and remained so until 1935.

Below: Looking up the inclined approach from Moreton Road in the 1950s, with the station entrance directly ahead. To the left is the rear wall of the up Woodside line platform, whilst the Oxted side, with its footbridge, appears on the right.

Right and below: Two views showing the Oxted line platforms on 28th July 1959, just over a month after they had closed. The top photograph looks south, whilst that below points north and includes the platforms serving the Woodside route on the right. The difference in levels between the two lines is emphasised by the way that the awning at centre stepped up. Interestingly, the posts supporting the canopies still sported the white painted banding, added to aid visibility during the Second World War blackouts.

Selsdon – 147

Above: Selsdon station viewed from a down train coming off the Woodside line on 28th April 1962, with the disused Oxted route platforms, still intact, on the left.

Left: A general view of the Woodside line platforms, seen from near the site of Selsdon Road North signal box. which had been abolished on 22nd September 1935. On the left, an ex-LBSCR Class C2x 0-6-0 is waiting to depart from the yard with an up goods train.

Right: Looking along the up Woodside line platform at Selsdon on an unknown date, with the stairs leading to the passenger subway on the left.

Below: Passengers accessing the station from its southern end did so by using the gate beside the building which is seen in this view dating from 23rd February 1963. Above this entrance is a white-on-green enamel sign stating *"Way In and Booking Office"*, although the latter adjoined the opposite platform and had to be reached by using the subway.

Above: The Woodside line platforms, looking north on 22nd February 1963. The south end of the up canopy, seen on the left, has been partially removed indicating that work on demolishing the Oxted side platform buildings was either under way or else completed.

Left: The booking office building survived the first phase of demolition, but probably not for long. This view, taken at an unknown date, shows its rear and includes the short flight of steps leading from the up Woodside platform. Above these, the nearest hanging sign states *"Way Out To Croham Road"*, whilst that a little further on directed passengers to the Booking Office.

After the remaining buildings had been demolished, BR erected short canopies above the stairs leading to the subway. This view looks towards the junction and includes the signal box in the distance.

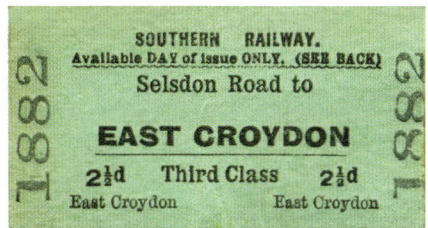

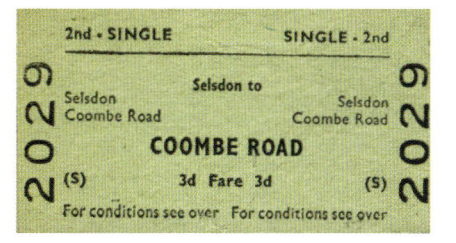

A selection of tickets: *Top left:* SR platform ticket issued on 19th March 195? (The final digit does not appear on the rear of the ticket) long after renaming. *Top centre:* SR Third Class single to East Croydon issued on 31st October 1944. *Top right:* SR Cheap Day ticket to South Croydon issued on 31st August 1938. *Bottom left:* Undated BTC Second Class single to Bingham Road. *Bottom centre:* BTC Second Class single to Coombe Road issued on 27th December 1962. *Bottom right:* Undated BTC platform ticket.

Selsdon – 151

Above: After the demolition of the booking office, British Railways provided replacement facilities in a small wooden hut on the down Woodside line platform. Here it is seen from the approach which led off Selsdon Road, with the stairway canopies visible on the right.

Left: A close-up view of the hut, with its ticket-issuing window protected by a small awning.

Right: A 2EPB unit arrives at Selsdon and is about to pass one of the white-on-green Southern Railway running-in boards which remained at the station well into the 1970s. Part of the little ticket hut is visible on the left.

Below: A 2-EPB leaves Selsdon and heads for Elmer's End in the 1970s, with one of the station's gas lamps prominent on the left.

Selsdon – 153

Above: Selsdon signal box in the 1970s, with the ramp of the disused up Oxted line platform on the right. Back then the cabin retained its white-on-green Southern Region nameboard, but this was changed to a corporate image British Rail sign soon after.

Left: The interior of Selsdon box taken around the same time, showing the levers and block instruments on the right. To the left, it is possible to see the down side stairway and its attendant canopy through the window behind the signalman's cooker.

154 – London's Disused Railway Stations – Outer South East London

Above: Even in bright sunshine, the station looked uninviting and desolate. Whereas both Bingham Road and Coombe Road generally had at least one member of staff on duty during service hours, the same couldn't be said for Selsdon, where the tatty ticket hut was invariably locked and shuttered. Here 2-EPB No 5767 stands at the down platform, awaiting its return to Elmers End.

Right: 2-EPB No 5725 rests at Selsdon prior to departing for Elmers End in 1983.

Selsdon – 155

Above: Selsdon signal box in March 1983, displaying the British Rail Corporate Image sign which replaced the earlier green vitreous enamel nameboard in the 1970s. The cabin outlived the station and remained in use until 1st April 1984.

Left: Looking south from the down Woodside line platform on the same date, with the junction on the left and the box to the right.

Right: An unusual view of the disused Oxted line platforms, showing the chemical toilet, complete with adjoining gas lamp, which was provided for staff use.

Below: Here we see the short flight of steps which connected the up Woodside and down Oxted line platforms, as they appeared on a wet afternoon shortly before Selsdon station closed completely.

Selsdon – 157

Above: Class 33 loco No 33053 is seen from Selsdon signal box whilst working an oil train. Although the majority of track along the Woodside line was lifted following closure in 1983, a stretch was retained at its southern end to allow access to the siding. However the facility was closed in March 1993 and the remaining track fell into disuse.

Left: The up side stairway canopy at Selsdon was removed following storm damage on 12th November 1977 and that on the down side followed later in the month. This handwritten poster was displayed on the ticket hut to inform passengers as to what had happened and what was about to happen.

Right: Some of the tickets which remained in the Selsdon booking hut at the time of closure in 1983.

After the stairway canopies were removed and their attendant walls reduced in height, the station began to look even more desolate than before. This view shows the down side in 1983, with a gas light glowing above one of the British Rail corporate image lamp tablets erected in the previous decade. It has been suggested that Selsdon was the last station in Greater London to be illuminated by gas and although this cannot be confirmed, it was certainly one of the last.

Selsdon – 159

Above: A view taken on the last day of passenger services as photographers record 2-EPB No 5763 departing for Elmers End. The former approach which once linked Croham and Moreton Roads with the original station booking office has disappeared amid the greenery on the right. The oil sidings which occupied the old goods yard were finally closed in March 1993.

Left: The overgrown Oxted line platforms at Selsdon, looking south on 3rd July 2019.